# SEEING LAW DIFFERENTLY

*Views From a Spiritual Path*

**Alan Reid**

**Borderland Publishing**

Portions reprinted by permission from *A Course in Miracles*. © 1975 Foundation for Inner Peace, Inc. and from *The Gifts of God*. © 1982 Foundation for Inner Peace, Inc.

Portions from *Les Miserables*, by Victor Hugo, are reprinted from *The Canadian Book of Prose and Verse*, Book Three. © 1932 The Ryerson Press and The MacMillan Company of Canada, Limited.

**Canadian Cataloguing in Publication Data**

Reid, Alan, 1942-
  Seeing law differently

Includes bibliographical references.
ISBN 0-9696039-0-8

1. Law - Philosophy. 2. Spiritual life. 3. Course in miracles. I. Title.

K240.R45 1992    340'.11    C92-090212-X

**To the Memory of my Father**

**COVER DESIGN:** The cover design, by Chandler Swain of Ottawa, Ontario, is the artist's impression of the author's image of the figure of Justice, seen differently. Traditionally seen as weighing truth impartially while blindfolded, Justice is here seen as removing her blindfold, setting down the scales, and seeing everyone's inherent innocence through forgiving eyes. The lilies she carries are used in *A Course in Miracles* as a symbol of forgiveness. The design portrays the essential connection between justice and forgiveness.

# CONTENTS

# FOREWORD

Several years ago, before either of us had come into contact with *A Course in Miracles*, my wife Barbara expressed the thought that someday I might write a book about law in the Golden Age. Although I treated it as an interesting suggestion, I had no idea what such a book might encompass. Nor do I presently.

Nonetheless, that thought was an inspiration for *this* book, which is about law in *this* age, and how a transformed vision of what law is *for* can bring healing to each of us and to our troubled world. For many, it will seem to be a radical vision of law and its function. Its emphasis on healing will be comforting to some, and will confront others.

The title "Seeing Law Differently" was the genesis of the book. Although it was used initially as the caption for a voluntary counselling program on law and spirituality, which Barbara and I ran in Ottawa for several months in 1989, I knew from the beginning that it would ultimately appear on the cover of this book. I began to write the book in 1990, then put it aside for a while before resuming it in the summer of 1991. Although the book was initially conceived to serve as a guide for others, I had not moved very far along in the writing before I realized that it was really about my own struggle with the meaning of law and my role as a lawyer. Only as I began to see a pattern emerging from working through my own process did the idea of sharing my thoughts with others surface once again as a realistic possibility.

The book makes a personal statement I could not have made without the encouragement and support of many with whom I shared the idea. Barbara, of course, has remained my chief confidante and supporter throughout, and without her vision, motivation and love I could not have expressed many of the comments I make in the book. But there have been many others. Val Scott opened my eyes to the possibility of there being a practical application of *A Course in Miracles* in the profession of law, and has given me strong encouragement, from the very first draft, as rough and incomplete as it was, to the final one. Chris Johnston, who is a friend, a lawyer and someone who deeply appreciates the beauty and value of *A Course in Miracles*, also read early drafts, and was able to help me see potential in the book that had thus far escaped me. He too has been a strong supporter throughout, in so many ways.

Several others have read various drafts, and have helped immeasurably along the way. I have had insightful comments from my friend Ernie Tannis, whom I think of as the Leo Buscaglia of the legal community. An eternally optimistic source of information about dispute resolution, Ernie has opened my eyes to the unlimited potential of love in a tough profession. I am grateful as well to my friend and colleague Catherine Kennedy, who, in reading early drafts with patience and understanding, came to learn and accept more about the lawyer she agreed to work with in 1989 than she would ever have imagined at the time.

My partner Allan O'Brien made an invaluable contribution, although he probably would not want to take credit for it. I trusted him to read, without judgment, two of my early drafts. Never having heard of *A Course in Miracles*, he obviously struggled with a lot of the concepts I was expressing. Still, he had a helpful way of raising questions that simply had to be addressed if the book was to have any meaning to persons outside the *Course* community.

I am indebted to Dr. Kenneth Wapnick and to Tom Gossett, two esteemed friends, both extremely knowledgeable about the *Course*, who took the time to read the draft manuscript carefully, and to provide me with extensive written comments about how the book might be strengthened. I am grateful for their insight and their warm encouragement.

There are many others to whom I wish to pay tribute for their contributions, some of whom will understand why, and others may not, although I assure them that I can explain should they ever ask. John Hunt, Mary Anne Buchowski-Monnin, Robert Perry, Bernard Lacroix, Tim Eastland, Bruce Judah, Lyman Purnell, Garry Rondeau, Bonnie Rondeau, Nan Benson, Janet Lee, Sunder and Rupinder Arora, Shari Culliver, Steve Gordon and Donald Neilson have all played roles in the unfolding of this project.

I want to mention as well my mother, Eleanor, and my late father, Elston, whose influences are referred to in the book, and, in particular, my son Geoffrey, whose sensitivity towards and interest in what his father was writing, at times about him, was a source of inspiration to me.

I want to express as well my gratitude for the invaluable contribution made by my secretary Joanne Martel, not only for the technical assistance she gave me in producing this book in form, but for her interest, understanding and support throughout the course of the project.

Finally, I want to acknowledge my friends Leanne and Maynard Dalderis, whose observation on our first meeting in 1988 that "there is a lot of room for healing in the legal profession" has stuck with me ever since. The wisdom expressed in their books is profound and deeply moving, and underlies much of what I communicate in this book.

My commitment to the teachings of *A Course in Miracles* is evident in the pages of the book. I want to express here my gratitude to the late Dr. Helen Schucman, the "scribe" of the *Course*, whose courage and dedication in her own project has inspired so many others, including my own. I also express my gratitude to the many authors who have written about the *Course*, for their contributions to my own modest understanding of the truth about what is real and what is illusory. I hope that this book, in turn, will inspire others to reflect upon their understanding of what is real and what is illusory, and help them to find the strength to share their insight with others.

A.R.

# INTRODUCTION

Let us be still an instant, and forget all things we ever learned, all thoughts we had, and every preconception that we hold of what things mean and what their purpose is. Let us remember not our own ideas of what the world is for. We do not know. Let every image held of everyone be loosened from our minds and swept away.

*A Course in Miracles*, Text, pages 602-3.

# MY VANTAGE POINT

This book is about my personal commitment to seeing law differently. It is also about my commitment to seeing the world differently. Although I have chosen law as my focus, because that is mainly what I do in the world, much of what I have to say applies equally to any other career path I might have chosen, whether it be medicine, teaching, counselling, music, sales or public administration - virtually any activity that brings us into relationship with others. For, essentially, my message is about functioning in a world of relationships, whatever our chosen role may be.

The book comes after my having spent more than twenty-five years as a lawyer, in a diverse career that has rewarded me with many interesting responsibilities and opportunities. I have had the privilege of studying at one of the world's great law schools. I was a law professor for a lengthy period. I worked for many years in government as a legislative draftsman, as a law reformer, and as a constitutional adviser and litigator. I served as a commissioner of the Law Reform Commission of Canada for three years. I have worked for the past several years in private practice as a partner in one of Canada's largest law firms. Over the years, I have written laws, taught them, reformed them, written about them and contested them, without ever *really* asking myself: What are these laws all about? What are they for? Is law about winning? Is it about control? Moral retribution? Fairness? Justice? Is law for peace? For love? For any or all of these? Why do people go to lawyers anyway? What is it they are seeking? And what does it mean to be a lawyer?

I have observed over the years that many people have an aversion to lawyers, to the law's process, and to the institutions within which law is administered. Most people I talk with have had at least one bad experience, either with the law or with a lawyer, and are only too eager to share it. For many, law is more frightening and intimidating than it is reassuring. It is a source of pain more than satisfaction, of stress more than comfort.

Many people today see the legal system in crisis. The cost of protecting people's rights has almost bankrupt some of the legal aid systems of the country. And without legal aid, it seems as though many legal services are priced beyond the reach of all but large corporations and wealthy individuals. A Task Force of the Canadian Bar Association[1] recently concluded that Canadians are losing faith in a court system they believe is too slow, too expensive and benefits mainly the rich and powerful. For the average person, resort to the law can be economically crippling.

As well, people are questioning how well the legal system really does protect people's rights, and how much justice is being dispensed. Do people have equal access to justice? Do people have equal access to legal information and services?

However legitimate those questions of access may be, the

---

[1]  *Report of the Canadian Bar Association Task Force on Court Reform in Canada*, Ottawa, Canada, August, 1991. In response to this report the Chief Justice of the Supreme Court of Canada requested the Canadian Judicial Council to initiate a study and to develop a plan to improve the efficiency of the court system at all levels.

legal system seems to be used more than ever. Increased use has clogged the courts, resulting in the need for more and more resources to meet the perceived needs of justice. Recently I heard it expressed informally by a judge that this may be because lawyers have done "too good a job" in defending and protecting people's rights. The law schools have trained law students *too well* to be sensitive to injustices. "Socially conscious" law professors have taught young lawyers to translate concerns about the social policy implications of specific events into legal arguments that courts will listen to. And there are so many lawyers out there, eager to attract clients and poised to advise them as to the ways in which they are being victimized by their spouses, their landlords, their employers, big corporations, the government and their neighbours, that the system is approaching overload. The problem is particularly acute in many of the states of the United States, to the point that legislatures are beginning to look at possible legislative amendments to deter what is widely seen as a tidal wave of frivolous litigation. It seems as though, despite the high costs of litigation, people still think of it as an appropriate way of dealing with their disputes.

The "crisis" also seems to take its toll at a more personal level. How many people truly feel well served by the legal system? Civil litigants find the process not only expensive, but physically and mentally draining, overly drawn out and generally frustrating. Whichever side they may be on, many feel attacked, vilified, manipulated, abused and exploited. Even the momentary sweetness of victory, whether as the successful instigator of proceedings or as a successful defendant, seems to be quickly displaced by the lingering pain of the stressful experience that must be undergone to achieve that moment of "success." Frequently the seeming victory dissipates in the wake of the exercise.

Most people, I think, tend to view law in terms of attack and defence. Law is there to be used to "get" what is rightfully theirs, to assert their rights against another person; or, it can be used to block someone else's attempt to get something from them. Lawyers usually advise clients to assume a defensive posture towards unnamed, but "reasonably foreseeable," strangers. These are the shadows that terrorize the ubiquitous "reasonable person," by whose standards legal responsibility is usually measured by courts. The "reasonable person" lives with the nightmare that any mistake may cause these shadows to manifest into plaintiffs, seeking redress for the "wrongs" inflicted by his or her errors in judgment. Seen from this perspective, law has much to do with attack, victimization, loss, lack and, of course, fear.

Most of us become fearful when we are on the receiving end of someone else's attempt to use the law against us. This may arise from something as simple as a parking or speeding ticket, or from being sued by someone, perhaps for a debt or for allegedly causing them injury when they slipped and fell on an icy driveway. It is not unusual to feel "attacked" in such circumstances, to bear resentment towards the person who is invoking the law against us, and to feel vulnerable to a process we do not understand and of which our experiences over a lifetime seem to reinforce our belief that we need be wary.

It is important to remember, as well, that the use of law may be no less fearful for the person who is "on the attack," i.e. the person who brings the suit against another, who lays a criminal charge against someone, or who sees the law as an appropriate means of resolving a family dispute. We think of law as a source of "protection" from other people, and thus as a way of responding to our fearful thoughts about the world we live in. We are taught that we should feel justified in using law to enforce our legal rights, thus to vindicate our sense of violation and outrage when someone else is perceived to have infringed our rights.

Feelings that surface within the *criminal* process can be particularly painful. The focus upon the "guilt" of the accused can engender feelings of revulsion within the community, feelings of rejection and resentment on the part of the accused person, and feelings of pain and embarrassment by family and friends. This can manifest in expressions of hostility towards the system, often towards the accused, and sometimes even towards the "victim." Much has been written about the plight of victims, who are often perceived as a sort of "fifth wheel" in the process, with little to say or do other than to nurture feelings of resentment towards everyone involved in the drama that has caused so much pain in their lives.

Is it surprising then that the legal process engenders so much negativity towards lawyers? Lawyers are often portrayed and retained as "gunslingers," whose job it is to make life difficult for the other side, to distort the truth, to manipulate the process, and to thwart any real opportunity for resolving the conflict. They are often perceived as "fixers," the sole benefactors of the process, objects of scorn, abuse and sometimes misplaced envy.

There is also growing discontent within the legal profession itself. There are many lawyers I know who do not really like what they do for a living. That is somewhat ironic in view of the arduous path one must pursue to enter the profession. There is stressful competition to gain admittance to law school. There is a grinding three year educational program involved in obtaining a degree, and a somewhat laborious prolongation of training in the articling period and bar admission courses. Law students scramble for "good" articling spots, only to find themselves competing for a decreasing number of hire-back positions. From the time the graduates of this process find employment and settle into the practice of law, their eyes become fixed on the partnership plateau, which is normally scaled around the end of six years of long hours and frantic billing. Failing to reach this plateau "on schedule" is often interpreted as failure and rejection.

The work that is assigned to young lawyers is often different than they had imagined or would have chosen. Lawyers quickly discover that the culture of legal practice is dominated by business values more than by service values. The quest seems to be to move beyond survival to prosperity, which comes through various combinations of hard work, expertise, notoriety, connections and good luck. And yet, in pursuing and maintaining the lifestyle, lawyers often find themselves trapped in work they either never liked or have grown tired of. Many corporate lawyers become bored with the sameness of their deal-structuring. Litigators often grow cynical from continuous stressful dealings with clients, judges and other lawyers.

The pent-up emotions arising from the stress or boredom of day to day routine are reflected in the relationships that represent the operation of the legal system. Ego runs rampant in the scramble to succeed or survive, and lawyers can lose sight of what the ideal of service to clients really entails. Stereotypes dominate the culture, and by and large the attack-defence syndrome shapes and nourishes those stereotypes. The legal culture is commonly seen to place a high value on competition and aggression; many within the profession come to believe that this is the way it must be. Some react by leaving the profession; some go on to become judges, a job that for many lawyers poses its own set of frustrations;[2] and others cope as best they can with their disillusionment. Still others, of course, do thrive and prosper as legal practitioners, finding fulfilment in what they do.

Many will dismiss the above as an overly simplistic analysis of legal culture, and fortunately my synopsis does not reflect everyone's experience. However, I think there is enough truth in it to make the general point that, by and large, lawyers are not a peaceful and happy lot in their work. To a large extent, the absence of peace, harmony and self-satisfaction in the legal profession simply mirrors a similar vacuum in society generally; there is a lot of unhappiness in the world. But does it have to be this way? Do we have our priorities in order?

In 1984, Warren Burger, then Chief Justice of the United States, in the Chief Justice's Annual Message on the

---

[2]    The Ottawa Citizen, on February 22, 1992, at p. A1, carried a report of a speech given on the previous day by Madame Justice Claire L'Heureux Dubé, of the Supreme Court of Canada, to a conference of judges in Halifax, Nova Scotia. Justice Dubé spoke of burn out, depression, stress-related sickness and alcoholism among judges, resulting from the significant pressures placed upon judges to resolve the difficult questions thrust upon them in the contemporary social context, particularly in light of the *Canadian Charter of Rights and Freedoms*.

Administration of Justice to the American Bar Association,[3] had some poignant things to say at the conclusion of a series of criticisms of the legal profession in the United States. He was largely centering on the propensity of lawyers in that country to litigate virtually any dispute, a propensity that some Canadian lawyers seem to be striving to emulate:

> We lawyers are creatures - even slaves - of precedent which is habit. We tend to do things in a certain way "because we have always done it that way." But when we must constantly witness spectacular expansions of court dockets, requiring more and more judges, something is wrong. When we see costs of justice rising, when we see our standing in public esteem falling, something is wrong.
>
> If we ask the question: "Who is responsible?", the answer must be "We are. I am. You are."
>
> The entire legal profession - lawyers, judges, law teachers - have become so mesmerized with the stimulation of the courtroom contest that we tend to forget that we ought to be healers - healers of conflicts. Doctors, in spite of astronomical medical costs, still retain a high degree of public confidence because they are perceived as healers. Should lawyers not be healers? Healers, not warriors? Healers, not procurers? Healers, not hired guns?

Only recently have I come to appreciate the enormous challenge that Chief Justice Burger presented to lawyers in that

---

[3]   This speech was given at the Midyear Meeting of the American Bar Association on February 12, 1984.

speech. He did not elaborate on what he meant by "healers," or how lawyers could become healers, but he signalled a need for each of us to look again at what it is we do. Writing this book is in part my response to that challenge. It is an undertaking on my part to share, not only with lawyers, but also with clients and with others who find themselves in relationships with lawyers, my understanding of how law can better serve to complement a process of healing,[4] what it means to have a "legal problem," how we can release the frustration that comes from being mired in the legal process, and, generally, how we can find greater satisfaction within the legal system, whatever our relationship to it may be. It is an invitation to all of us to re-examine our expectations about how law and the legal system can solve our problems, to accept personal responsibility for the ways in which we experience the system from our various points of view, and to look honestly at the suggestion that each one of us, through the ways in which we perceive and use law, contributes to the so-called "crisis" in the legal system about which we like to complain.

In a broad sense, this is a book about law reform. My experience on the Law Reform Commission of Canada taught me the valuable lesson that law reform is only in part about changing the letter and form of our laws. Law reform, I learned, is as much about changing attitudes as it is about changing laws. As I have moved through subsequent experiences, both in law and otherwise, I have been attracted increasingly towards a personal, more so than an institutional,

---

[4]     The idea of healing that I present in this book is the subject of Part I. Essentially, it is the healing of the conflict in our minds through the practice of forgiveness.

commitment to attitudinal change. I have come to believe that better laws, better law administration and true justice start with a forgiving attitude to each other, to our society and to ourselves. My current focus on law reform is what I would describe as the "reform" of how we look at law, how we use it, and what we use it for, as lawyers, clients, judges, legislators, businesspersons and ordinary citizens. I see the commitment to healing, of which I have just spoken, as a principal focus of law reform. It's not that I think we should stop doing things that can help make a better atmosphere in which healing can occur. It's that attitudinal change must precede and accompany whatever efforts and decisions are taken in the name of change.

Having subtitled this book "Views From a Spiritual Path," I feel it is appropriate at this juncture to say something about my concept of a "spiritual path," and about my own spiritual path and how it relates to the idea of healing. My understanding of a "spiritual path" is that it is a set of beliefs about ourselves as spiritual beings. I think of it as being more personal than a "religion," which tends to involve infrastructure, institutions, officials and doctrine, and which usually requires that one commit oneself to a kind of political movement built around a spiritual belief. While many people find their spiritual paths within a religion, that has not been my experience.

There is no such thing as a "right" or a "wrong" spiritual path. It is about finding what works for you, what brings you into a keener awareness of your spiritual reality and a feeling of closeness with God. I am not using "God" in any particular religious sense, but rather in the sense of our Source of Being, perfect Love, the Truth that lies beyond our limited perception, a beneficent Divine Presence in every human heart,[5] all of which I believe we have the capacity to be in touch with, if we choose to be. Every path, if it is truly a spiritual one, leads its traveller home eventually.

My spiritual path began in the autumn of 1987, when a series of personal experiences led me to begin to read a set of books entitled *A Course in Miracles*.[6] No writing has so profoundly affected my view of the world. I mention this, not to promote it as a path, but to explain to readers where I am in making the observations about law and the legal system that I make in this book. *A Course in Miracles* has taught me that I,

---

[5] This latter phrase, "a beneficent...," which I find to be a beautiful expression of the presence of God within each of us, I have borrowed from the Affirmations and Principles of the New Seminary, an Institute dedicated to the training of Interfaith Ministers, spiritual counsellors and practitioners to teach, counsel and work in the community. The New Seminary is based in New York, N.Y., U.S.A.

[6] *A Course in Miracles* was "scribed" by Dr. Helen Schucman, a clinical psychologist at the Columbia-Presbyterian Medical Center in New York City, over a seven year period that began in 1965 (which, coincidentally, was the year of my graduation from law school and admission to the bar). The books are published and distributed by the Foundation for Inner Peace, Glen Ellen, California, U.S.A. First published in 1976, there are presently 750,000 copies in circulation in the English speaking world. Versions in Spanish and Portuguese are expected in 1993, and plans are in various stages of progress to have the books translated into twelve other languages, including French. The story of the coming into being of the *Course* is told in the recent biography of Helen Schucman by the preeminent scholar of *A Course in Miracles*, Dr. Kenneth Wapnick, *Absence from Felicity* (New York, 1991).

not God and not anyone "out there" in the world, am responsible for how I experience the world. It has helped me to train myself to look at my relationships differently, and in particular to look at and release the grievances and judgment I harbour that distort my perceptions of reality. The "miracle," in the title of the *Course*, is essentially the shift in perception we experience when we look at any situation with love[7] in our hearts, and without the fear and guilt our egos customarily allow to shape our perceptions of people, things, events and situations.

Although expressed predominantly in Christian terminology, *A Course in Miracles* reflects currents of both Eastern and Western spiritual thought in presenting its unique form of the universal spiritual curriculum. Although Jesus has a major role in its teachings, the *Course* is not generally thought of as part of the mainstream Christian movement. The *Course* presents the idea of God as a loving, not a vengeful presence. It looks upon "evil" only as a belief we hold onto, not as part of Reality. It recognizes each one of us, along with Jesus, as a

---

[7]   I use the words "Love","love" and "loving" in this book to convey the notion of Being, or Reality, being in touch with Truth, or in a state of Peace. In the Introduction to *A Course in Miracles* it is stated that: "The course does not aim at teaching the meaning of love, for that is beyond what can be taught. It does aim, however, at removing the blocks to the awareness of love's presence, which is your natural inheritance." This awareness comes with our willingness to release the illusions of fear and guilt, and our openness to "miracles," which are corrections in our thinking, not the supernatural occurrences that are commonly associated with that word in day to day usage. We experience miracles when we look at any situation in a state of "right-mindedness," which is our remembrance of and attunement to Love.

Child of God, Jesus being the symbol of the potential in each of us to remember our spiritual connections with God and with each other. Not only Jesus but all of us make up "the Christ," the experience of which enables us to see the world in a different light.

Because its thought system expresses such a powerful psychology, the *Course* is sometimes described as a meeting ground of psychology and spirituality. It explains the complex and deeply seated belief we have in the ego, and how the ego works to keep from us an awareness of the true nature of God and of our relationship with God. Stripped to its essentials, the *Course*'s message is this: Our seeming "reality," the "world" we experience, is the product of how we think. We can think in an emotional state of fear and anger; or we can think in a state of love, remembering that beneath the veneer of appearances we are all calling out for help and for love. Our lives and all our experiences are about a search for inner peace, about releasing the guilt and fear we walk around with each day. The choice to heal the conflict that haunts us is there for each of us to make, repeatedly, continuously, in every situation we encounter. Free will is the freedom to make that choice.

The most helpful tool we can use for healing is "forgiveness," a key concept in *A Course in Miracles*, but used in a way that differs from common usage. To "forgive" is essentially to look at what we think has happened and to recognize that nothing we perceive is as it appears to be. We see everything through the filters of our minds, coloured by our judgments, our prejudices, our values, our fears, our past experiences and by our strong attachment to being right. What we think has happened is a product of interpretation. It is an illusion. From a lawyer's perspective, the first step in the process of forgiveness is not unlike the realization every good trial lawyer has that there is no such thing as a truly reliable witness. People see what they choose to see.

The thread that ties together the ideas I explore in this book is this concept of "forgiveness." It is not the forgiveness of one who "pardons" another for a crime or misdemeanour. "Pardon" implies a prior judgment that the one who is pardoned has truly committed the crime or misdemeanour. Instead, the forgiveness of which I speak involves recognizing that we are in a constant state of judgment about someone or something, and choosing to let this judgment go in order to see the person or the situation in a spiritual light.

One of the beautiful stories I like to use to illustrate forgiveness is the one Victor Hugo tells in *Les Miserables* of Jean Valjean's encounter with the Bishop. In this story, Jean, only days before, has been released from his nineteen years in prison (the first five years for stealing a loaf of bread to feed his family, and the last fourteen years for his repeated, unsuccessful efforts to escape). When he arrives at the Bishop's door the servants are in a state of fear, having heard reports of an unseemly stranger in the area. The Bishop, in a state of total defencelessness, invites Jean to dine with him, insisting that the best silver be set to celebrate the presence of his guest. The Bishop is undaunted by Jean's repeated voicings of his expectation that he will be turned away because he is a convict. Jean, not appreciating that he is in the presence of the Bishop, is greatly moved by the acceptance and respect that is extended to him by this person, whom he believes to be only the curé. The Bishop addresses Jean as "Sir," and openly refers to him as his "brother."

After supper, the Bishop hands Jean a silver candlestick and shows him to a room and bed with fresh linen. Unaccustomed to the comfort of a bed, Jean wakes up during the night and succumbs to the temptation to help himself to the silver. When the Bishop is confronted the next morning by Madame Magloire, who informs him that their "guest" has disappeared with "our" silver, he replies: "By the way, was that plate ours? ... Madame Magloire, I had wrongfully held back this silver, which belonged to the poor. Who was this person? A poor man evidently." The Bishop continued in this vein when the local gendarmes arrived shortly thereafter with Jean in tow. Speaking to Jean he said: "Ah, there you are! ... I am glad to see you. But how is this? Why, I gave you the candlesticks, too, which are also silver, and will fetch you two hundred francs. Why did you not take them away with the forks and spoons?" The Bishop again offered the candlesticks to Jean as the gendarmes were releasing him. Jean was totally bewildered and speechless. The Bishop then continued: "Do not forget. Never forget that you have promised to use this money in becoming an honest man. ... Jean Valjean, my brother, you no longer belong to evil, but to good. I have bought your soul of you. I withdraw it from black thoughts and the spirit of perdition and I give it to God."

What is remarkable about the story, to my mind, is that the Bishop truly did not see Jean as a sinner or as a criminal. He saw the events in a fundamentally different light than did Madame Magloire, the onlooker. The Bishop was coming from love and acceptance; Madame Magloire was coming from fear. His paradigm was spiritual unity; hers was separation.

Jean, in succumbing to the temptation to steal the silver, had merely acted out the role that he had come to accept was assigned to him by society. He had made every effort to convince the Bishop to see him as a convict, which was how he had convinced himself that everyone saw him to be. Through the metaphor of the Bishop buying Jean's soul with the silver, Hugo illustrated the healing power of forgiveness. Jean began to see himself as did the Bishop. Through the vision of the Bishop, he was released; he was truly free.

To me the story is a beautiful illustration of transformation through vision, of the healing power of love overcoming the limiting effect of judgment. The story stresses how the paradigm shift, the "miracle," releases us from the perceptions that imprison us in our beliefs about pain and suffering. The Bishop could have used the law to attack Jean Valjean for the "crime" he had committed. However, he chose to see differently. The choice he made was that of true forgiveness, and only with that choice was he able to truly serve him as a brother.

Not all stories of forgiveness have such happy outcomes, which we tend to equate with the "success" of our decisions to forgive. It is important to emphasize, not only in relation to the story I have just outlined but to all stories of forgiveness, that forgiveness is a choice made by those who forgive in support of their own healing, not that of the one who is forgiven. The Bishop's forgiveness of Jean was part of his own healing process. The healing Jean experienced involved choices of his own. Not always do those whom we forgive make the choice for healing, and the outcomes, if measured in terms of the object of forgiveness, will not always satisfy our expectations of change for the better.

Writing this book has been an important part of my own process of healing. In recent years I have struggled a great deal to understand my role as a lawyer (many new friends look incredulously at me when I tell them what I do for a living). Can law be reconciled with healing? Is it possible to see it differently? This book is my attempt to address those questions. It is an attempt to find a meeting ground for spiritual and legal principles. In subsequent discussion, I look at law and at related concepts such as conflict, conflict resolution, legal rights, legal obligations, fault, guilt and innocence, justice and punishment through my spiritual lens, to explore the meaning of those concepts and how they relate to healing. I consider how professionals working within the system, particularly lawyers, can help to facilitate the healing of "legal consumers." In this respect, I also focus on the opportunities lawyers are given to heal their own conflict as they deliver professional services to clients.

The dominant idea I express while looking at those issues is that every experience we have in life, and every person we meet, offers to us the opportunity to forgive, i.e. to see differently, and through this to heal ourselves and, in healing ourselves, to heal others.[8] *A Course in Miracles* reminds us that

---

[8] Strictly speaking, we cannot heal others. Only they can make the choice for healing. When I speak in this book about "healing others" I do not mean to suggest that healing is something I can *do to someone else*. Nor is forgiveness, which is the vehicle for healing, really about doing. It is about looking and seeing; there are no behavioral imperatives. The healing of which I speak is on the level of the mind, and it is on that level that my healing influences and facilitates the

our essential purpose in the world is to learn the lesson of forgiveness. We forgive whenever we are willing to look at a situation as would the loving Bishop, putting aside our propensity to judge and getting in touch with our remembrance of God's love. Those are ideas that can be applied in the context of the law and the legal system as readily as they can be applied in education, health care, social services, public administration and day to day living. I can choose to stop looking at law as a means of judging and attacking others. I can choose to see law and to use it differently, in aid of true conflict resolution. The fundamental question about every experience is this: Is it about judgment or is it about healing? How I answer that question, and the responsibility I accept for the answer I choose, shapes all my experiences. It says everything about the meaning laws and legal institutions have for me, and how I relate to them.

Seeing law differently is to accept that law, for the most part, reflects ideas people have about how to facilitate and regulate our relationships and our interactions with others. They are often based on fearful thoughts, and so they may seem sometimes to exacerbate and frustrate these relationships and interactions. It is easy to locate the source of our problems in the law itself. I have come to recognize, however, that when I feel that law and the legal system is generating conflict in me, or is getting in the way of healing, it is time to change my mind

---

healing of others. Expressed metaphysically, the healing of my mind contributes to the healing of other minds because minds are joined. Expressed in a worldly sense, my healing serves as a light to others to recognize their choice for healing. These ideas will be developed more fully in Part I, in the section "Law as an Opportunity for Healing."

about what I am seeing. It is a sign that I am giving to the law a power over me that it does not have. In most cases the conflict I feel is related to how I am looking at the situation, or at the law as I think it applies to the situation, or at the people with whom I am interacting. When I begin to feel conflicted, it is time to look hard at what it is I am feeling.

In walking through my professional world on my spiritual path, I have come to the following realizations, which I explore in more depth as I progress through this book:

- That by looking at my attachment to judgment and at how I use law as a means of attack and defence, I can open myself to the opportunity law offers for healing conflict.
- That a different way of understanding the nature and essence of "conflict" helps me to see how law, like anything else, offers an opportunity for healing.
- That "rights" and "obligations," understood in a spiritual context, can be aids to healing rather than sources of conflict.
- That I can look at legal concepts such as "fault" and "guilt" without judging someone's real worth.
- That I can look at "justice" and "injustice" and at "punishment" in a way that does not perpetuate the belief that we are living in a society of victims and victimizers, a psychological state that is not conducive to healing.
- That the lawyer/client relationship presents me with repeated opportunities for healing. How I respond to these opportunities has an important bearing on how effectively I serve my clients.
- That forgiveness can bring healing into every corner of the legal system.

- That in making a commitment to healing I can find happiness and fulfilment in what I do for others as a lawyer.

This last point is particularly important, because it provides a clue as to why I should want to see law and the legal system in the functional light of healing. Robert Perry, in a recent article,[9] has expressed the thought that "only by being a light to the world, only by healing others," are we provided with "the proof our minds need within a world of hate, attack, guilt and death, that there is Something in us not of this world." It "increases our concept of being." Healing, then, provides us with a taste of who we really are and welcome relief from our spiritual hunger and thirst, which goes largely unsatisfied by our relationships, our careers, our worldly accomplishments, the possessions we accumulate and the power and control we feel justified in wielding over others. Healing through forgiveness is a path back to sanity.

Healing is also a contribution I can make to a more loving and compassionate world. It is not to seek to change the world, or anything or anybody in the world, in any specific way. To pursue that goal would be to endorse the belief that the problems and conflict we experience in the world have their source outside our minds, which runs counter to the ideas that support the observations I make about law in this book. And yet, as we carry our light into the world in whatever it is we do we elevate the general awareness of love's presence and allow

---

[9]     This article, entitled "The Earthly Extension," appears in the newsletter *Insight*, Volume Two - Number Three, September 1991, published by the Insight Foundation for ACIM, Ganges B.C., Canada.

for the experience of change in the world. Overall, I believe that the most fundamental and functional contribution we can make is to commit ourselves, individually and collectively, to removing the obstacles we have placed in the way of our awareness of the presence of love, which is our life force. Those obstacles are erected by us in the psychological state of fear we have assumed in our mistaken belief that we are spiritually separated from each other and from God.

Fundamental to my seeing law differently is my belief that I am under no laws but the laws of God.[10] In using that expression I do not allude to the Ten Commandments God reputedly handed down to Moses on the mountain. I think of those as laws of the world, as ancient precursors of our modern legal systems. Rather, I use the phrase "laws of God" in reference to the idea of our spiritual unity and the state of Love as our natural and real state. Everything I do in the world, including the practice, application and making of law, is subordinate to that overriding thought. It is not that we are to ignore the laws of the world, but that we are free to choose to make, administer and apply them from a loving, not a fearful, perspective. That is the meaning I choose to attribute to the idea expressed in the preamble to the *Canadian Charter of Rights and Freedoms* that Canada "is founded upon principles that recognize the supremacy of God and the rule of law." I make a special point, later in this book, of addressing how spiritual principles can be related to constitutional law, with particular emphasis on how forgiveness can bring healing in the process of constitutional

---

[10] This is a restatement of Lesson 76 in the Workbook of *A Course in Miracles*, "I am under no laws but God's."

reform.

In saying all that, I accept that I can only speak for myself and commit myself to looking at law differently. There are assumptions I make that may not be embraced by all readers. I am writing from my own experience, and I express only my own vision about reconciling my role as a lawyer with my spiritual path. And while I write exclusively from the vantage point of *my* path, *A Course in Miracles*, I recognize that there are many paths that converge at the door of spiritual awakening. Nonetheless, in sharing my thoughts, I offer the opportunity to others, whether now or at some future time, to choose to open themselves to the possibility of "seeing law differently." For all those who at some point have expressed in one form or another the thought that "there has to be a better way...," I offer my vision of another legal world.

In extending that offer, I can envisage things coming up for readers as they work through this book that may be difficult to deal with. Those who are not familiar with the thought system of *A Course in Miracles* may have difficulty understanding some of the terminology I use, although I endeavour as best I can to explain unconventional usage where it occurs. Beyond language is the realm of ideas. Many of the thoughts expressed in this book could give rise to strong reactions, especially by lawyers. My expression of such ideas as lawyers "forgiving" their clients, my vision of the "innocence" of "criminals," my focusing on spiritual responses to physical violence and my downplaying of "winning" may tempt some readers to throw away the book, dismissing the ideas as the ravings of someone who has "lost his perspective." I admit that my perspective has shifted. However, I do not believe in "loss" any more than I believe in the answers that the law and the legal system have traditionally offered as solutions to the conflict that people experience.

I invite those who read this book to look carefully at what it brings up for them, and to search within themselves for at least a little willingness to see differently. Those who find within themselves the willingness to look at how pervasively the ego thought system has invaded the world of law, as it has the other worlds of our experience, may find themselves asking how well what they do in those worlds serves the goal of healing. The chapters that follow are intended more to assist in framing the question than in providing an answer. In the end, both the question and the answer are expressed in the idea of choice - am I willing to make the choice to see differently? Am I willing at least to recognize that there is a choice? Am I willing to be in touch with my spiritual essence and to see beyond the veil that obscures the vision of Justice?

Seeing law differently does not mean that I no longer experience fear and its related emotions as situations confront me. I am constantly in and out of fear. It does, however, show me a way to move beyond the fear and the limitations we impose upon ourselves in acting out our fears. In simply standing back and observing what is going on, and how we allow fear to block our view of truth, we are taking the first step towards freeing ourselves from the prisons we have made. Those who are at least open to the possibility of there being "another way of looking at the world"[11] and of looking at the use of law in the

---

[11] This is a reference to a theme developed more fully in Part IV - Context.

world may be sufficiently intrigued to follow me on my journey through this book.

# PART I - HEALING

*Healing*

To heal it is not needful to allow
The thought of bodies to engulf your mind
In darkness and illusions. Healing is
Escape from all such thoughts. You hold
instead
Only a single thought, which teaches you
Your brother is united with your mind,
So bodily intrusions on his peace
Cannot arise to jeopardize the Son
Whom God created sinless as Himself.
Think never of the body. Healing is
The thought of unity. Forget all things
That seem to separate. Your brother's pain
Has but one remedy; the same as yours.
He must be whole, because he joins with you,
And you are healed, because you join with
him.

Helen Schucman, 1971. From *The Gifts of God*, page 27.

## LAW AS AN OPPORTUNITY FOR HEALING

I had idealistic impressions of the law when I was growing up. My mother had been a legal secretary, and my father's ambition had been to become a lawyer. I was an impressionable twelve years old when I first thought that my "calling" in life was to carry out my father's unfulfilled ambition. I devoured books that celebrated the glamour of the law. I identified with the nobility of the idea of justice, as I then understood it. The law was about right and wrong, good and evil, justice and injustice. Law was for crusaders, for the righteous, for those who wished to do good in the world.

I should also disclose that, for many of the same reasons, I also had a secret attraction to becoming a minister. I was brought up in the Anglican Church, was a choir boy and an altar boy, and genuinely felt that I had some appreciation of and insight into the teachings of Jesus. However, about the time I was fifteen years of age, for reasons I do not entirely recall other than my emergence into what I then understood to be my intellectual maturity, I rejected the church and its teachings for more secular philosophies, and lived the next thirty years of my life, sometimes as a confident atheist and sometimes as a cautious agnostic.[12] Given my philosophical state at the time

---

[12] I recently heard it expressed, and it certainly accords with my own experience, that people who call themselves atheists are not really denying the existence of God, but rather are denying the image of "God" that they grew up with. That image is of the ego. The Judeo-Christian God that many of us grew up with is the projection of the ego, with the same anger, judgment and attraction to special love and special hate that we all experience in the world. We created God in *our* image,

I was choosing my career, law seemed a natural vehicle for me to use to express my desire to serve.

The vision of law that drew me to it as a career was not an uncommon one. Most people, I suspect, see law as a force to protect them, to uphold the interests of the right and innocent, and to punish wrongdoers. And yet, almost always it seems to fall short of meeting those expectations. People are not always protected, innocent people seem to suffer, and even the "winners" seem to lose, judging by the anguish so many of them endure in their efforts to recover for what they think someone else has done to them contrary to law.

Why does the legal system bring so much pain? Is there something inherently wrong in the idea of law and legal institutions? Is the system permeated with corruptness, incompetence or both? Or could it be that the problem is the attitudes we, as individuals and as a society, hold, not just toward the system itself, but to the perceived "problems" we have that give rise to our resort to the system? How, when and why people use law to resolve their "problems" has a great deal to do with how they look at them from a spiritual and psychological perspective, and with their expectations about what legal process will do to solve them. People tend to forget or to overlook that perceived "legal problems" are only human problems with a legal component. I have become convinced that

---

not the other way around. Rather than moving on to a more mature understanding of God, as I would in probing the nature of a fundamental legal concept, I chose to reject the reality of God in favour of the constructs of my own intellect. From what I have heard others express, I have come to recognize that mine was not an uncommon experience.

solving the relationship difficulties that underlie most, if not all, "legal problems" has little to do with solving the so-called legal aspects of the problem.

For some people, it may *seem* enough to deal with the legal aspects of their "problems." From my perspective, however, both the "legal problem" and the "legal solution" are illusory. Almost always they mask more fundamental problems and solutions that we, both individually and as a society, are unable or unwilling to look at. The fear and frustration people experience with the law and with lawyers is a manifestation of this inability or unwillingness to deal with their "legal problems" as issues about relationships. People try to use law to resolve problems the law is incapable of resolving. They try to pass over to lawyers their own responsibility for addressing these problems. Many lawyers readily agree, and some even encourage clients to do this. In doing so, the problem is shifted onto an illusory battleground.

Suppose law could be seen not as a means of control exerted by winners over losers, not as a weapon of attack and vengeance, not as a basis of judgment, but rather as a process that can really draw the community and its members together, to help the community function more smoothly and to reduce the fear and animosity that are expressed in anti-social behaviour. Suppose we could begin to appreciate that law need not be a divisive influence, splitting communities and families into factions, and promoting labelling, stigmatization and a view of the world as separated into victims and victimizers. Suppose law and legal process could be seen differently, as an opportunity for forgiveness, for healing and for coming into touch with a true sense of community. As Helen Schucman has reminded us in the poem recited at the beginning of this Part, "Healing is the thought of unity."

The thought of unity is more than a nice thought. It is an essential thought if we are truly committed to peace in our lives and in the world. Healing is looking at love extending through us and seeing it joined with the love we are willing to see in others. As long as we believe we are separated from others, as long as we project blame onto others for what we perceive to be our problems, we close the door to healing. The peace of my brothers and sisters is *my* concern, because it is also *my* peace. When I use the law to attack them, I reinforce conflict and hold peace at bay. Peace and conflict are irreconcilable pursuits.

Seeing law differently for me is to choose healing over judgment and attack. I choose healing when I am willing to take another look at the moral indignation I hold towards those who deviate from the law. I choose healing when I am willing to question my attachment to my views about the world and about particular situations, people and events I experience in it. It is by looking at these attachments, and at the controls I exert to maintain them, that I work at healing my conflicts.

I should say a few words at this point about "attachments," in case readers should suddenly have felt their identities come under attack. Most of us feel strongly about certain things. We often refer to this as having "principles" and "values." People are often unwilling to give up or to compromise them, preferring to stand up and be counted. When we think about it, however, our principles and values often just reflect our beliefs about our upbringing, our past experiences, our social and cultural conditioning and what we have been taught. They can be a source of strength, but they can also be a source of conflict for us. We may have to defend and justify them to others, to rationalize them to ourselves and to renew again and again our faith in them. Our reluctance to let them go is often fear-based. What would we do without our principles and values? Our egos, reputations and self images are attached to and are dependent upon them. And yet, our principles and values often keep us in a state of conflict.

One of the teachings of *A Course in Miracles* is that healing comes only with our willingness to question all the values that we have ever learned about living in the world.[13] It is not that we should not have values and principles; it is that we should ensure that they are love-based, not fear-based. Our values are fear-based when they reinforce our desire to judge others (in the sense of condemning or finding fault with them). They are love-based when they help us reach out to people where they're at, regardless of how bad the objective circumstances may seem to be. If we are at peace with our principles and values, if we are not feeling compelled to defend them or to use them to attack others, then we are no longer "attached" to them. We accept them as part of us, as serving us, as helping us to see beyond the conflict we were tempted to reinforce with our use of law and the legal system. If we are in this state of consciousness, then the stresses of the law and the legal system will not be part of our experience. "I am under no laws but God's" will be the principle that serves as our path to healing.

Legal disputes usually involve a disagreement about

---

[13] *A Course in Miracles*, Text, p.464.

facts, or about the meaning of a law and how it applies to the facts, or both. It is a matter of one side seeing the situation one way, and the other side seeing it differently. This invariably brings up conflict in both. And yet, it offers both sides the chance and the choice to really look at that conflict and to see beyond it. The fact that the legal process has been engaged can serve to imprison or to release us. We can look upon it as an opportunity for healing, and make a commitment to healing, or we can see it as a problem, rejecting the opportunity to go beyond appearances. Every encounter with the law provides us with the opportunity to look at the attachments we have to our positions. Those attachments block our readiness for healing and for release from the state of conflict in which we find ourselves.

Popular perceptions of law see it working in the opposite direction. Law is seen as a way of *reinforcing* our attachments to our positions. Thus, the legal system becomes a battleground in which each combatant seizes upon the law as a weapon to attack and control his or her perceived adversary. To begin to see law as an opportunity for healing requires a 180 degree shift in perception about its function. Only when we can see law and legal process functioning as an aid to *releasing* us from our attachments to the positions we use to attack others, rather than *reinforcing* those attachments, can we begin to resolve our perceived conflicts.

This process of resolution is greatly assisted if we make it *our* process, by accepting responsibility for it. Although others can help us, no one else can resolve the conflicts that we experience.

A recent request from a friend brought me squarely into touch with the potential for healing that lies hidden in our so-called legal problems. Gerry had left his wife Cynthia about three years earlier, after some seventeen years of marriage. He was embarking on a spiritual journey Cynthia was unwilling to join. Feeling guilty about his choice to leave his wife and teenaged children, Gerry had proposed a separation agreement containing unusually stringent support commitments that he undertook to Cynthia on her own behalf and on behalf of the children. This agreement eventually became part of their divorce arrangements.

Not long after the divorce, Gerry married Brenda, who became his wife and spiritual partner. Gerry continued to honour his commitments to Cynthia and his children. He had a good paying job, and though it was difficult to make the support payments he continued to do so. He was even content to overlook certain facts that might have entitled him to withhold support under the terms of the agreement.

Two things led to my involvement in the situation. First, Gerry's wife Brenda had opened a spiritually oriented business that was becoming a focus of their life together. Gerry helped Brenda in the business during his leisure hours, and began to see exciting opportunities for making significant changes in his life. Second, he began to acknowledge openly how dissatisfied he was with his present job, despite the good income he was able to earn from it. Gerry and Brenda began to visualize a long term plan that would free Gerry to leave his job, to work with Brenda full-time in the business, and to join Brenda in developing and implementing plans to expand into related areas of spiritual healing.

Matters began to unfold more quickly than anyone had imagined. Gerry was quite open about his plans, sharing them with many people, including his former wife, Cynthia, and his employer. Cynthia immediately turned over to the provincial enforcement agency the task of collecting the support payments from Gerry. Gerry's employer "invited" Gerry to leave his position much earlier than Gerry had thought he would resign; Brenda was unable to sell her home, which was an important element of the plan to reduce the cost of day to day living. Quite understandably, Gerry became very concerned about what might happen when he found himself without the means to continue paying support.

During this period, Gerry and I had talked about some of the legal implications of these changes in his life, and whether he would be able to obtain from a court a "variance" of the support agreement. Gerry's idea of a "variance" was the total cessation of what was a contingent lifetime commitment to support Cynthia, and an extended support obligation in favour of the children. As a lawyer, I had told him that the circumstances that were described in the agreement as justifying variance were likely not met in his situation, and that his inability to pay might not be seen sympathetically by a judge, particularly if the judge saw Gerry as having left his job voluntarily. That would not be an unreasonable view of the situation. Although a downward adjustment of support might be possible, in view of all the circumstances a court would not likely make an order that would effectively end the agreement he had made with Cynthia. Besides, if Cynthia consulted her lawyer there would likely be a vigorous contest, and, from what Gerry had told me, I knew he did not want to open up old wounds.

The problem was that events had overtaken Gerry, and he found himself in a position that 1) he could not comply with the agreement, and 2) he felt morally right about ending it. He felt he had conceded to Cynthia the lion's share of the property at the time of the separation, that he had supported her through a relationship with another man (which he had not been obliged to do under the agreement), that she was in a relatively good financial situation with a reasonably good paying job, and that he had supported his children when they needed it most; now they were both able and willing to assume more responsibility for their own support. Furthermore, he had reached an understanding with his children about ending their support. From his standpoint, what could reasonably be seen as a transitional arrangement from one life situation to another had fulfilled its purpose.

Gerry wanted to write to Cynthia to inform her that, as of a specified date, there would be no further support cheques. When he consulted me about the letter, I suggested that he prepare a first draft himself, which we could go over together and modify as necessary. It was only when I reviewed his draft that I came fully into touch with the feeling that my role was not to advise him, as a lawyer ordinarily might, to refrain from sending the letter, or to modify it to avoid potential legal liabilities should Cynthia choose to use the letter against him. What impressed me was that the letter was beautifully sensitive, genuine, from the heart and filled with love. Still, something was troubling me about it that I was unable to put my finger on.

I asked Barbara, my wife, to read the letter, a step I was confident that Gerry would be agreeable to. Barbara's feeling, upon reading the draft, was that Cynthia would be upset with the letter, primarily because it offered nothing to her. It was a unilateral ending of the support relationship, an announcement by

Gerry of a *fait accompli*. We could both foresee Cynthia angrily turning the matter over to the enforcement officials for them to deal with. The letter, though sensitive in many ways, invited no healing, either for Gerry or for Cynthia. Barbara and I spent most of the afternoon discussing the letter. What could Gerry say that might precipitate healing?

What was coming to both of us was this: the one thing Gerry was in a position to extend to Cynthia in a loving way, apart from reassurances of his commitment to the children should they ever really need help from him, was a request that she release him from the agreement and forgive him for all the grievances she was holding against him. The forgiveness requested was really for Cynthia, not for Gerry. Although it was for Cynthia to choose whether or not to see it this way, we agreed that the request to release Gerry from the agreement and from the bonds of the relationship was the most valuable thing that he could offer her in the present circumstances. But only if Cynthia was willing to see it as an opportunity to forgive could she receive the gift of healing.

It was a simple matter for me to jot down our ideas about completing Gerry's letter. The words flowed from spirit. They were hidden in the lines Gerry had himself written, before he became blocked in the last paragraph. But would Gerry accept our suggestions? Was he willing to experience the release and forgiveness that the letter demanded on his part? Could he look beyond the attachment he had to the correctness of his legal position and ask Cynthia to release him from an obligation that he considered he no longer owed?

When Barbara and I approached Gerry about the letter, we first suggested that he think about what he might offer

Cynthia. His initial reaction was that he had not intended to offer her anything. Then we talked about the experience Barbara and I had gone through with the letter. Ultimately, I read to Gerry our suggestions for the additional paragraphs. As I read the words he began to cry, openly, unabashedly, and from the heart. We knew that this was what he truly wanted to say to Cynthia, and that he wanted for her the gift of healing. In that moment he himself received the gift. All three of us shared in a healing that afternoon as we read and discussed the letter. The love and forgiveness that Barbara and I felt towards Gerry, towards Cynthia whom we had never met, and towards each other as we identified with the feelings that surrounded this situation, brought healing to us as well.

Each of us understood that we had to release any attachment we had to the outcome of the letter. As much as we hoped that Cynthia, upon receiving the letter, would share in the healing we had experienced, it was her choice to accept or to reject the opportunity that Gerry's letter represented. Our own healing could not be conditional on Cynthia's acknowledgment of Gerry's request for forgiveness, if the request was truly an expression of love.

Gerry called me two days later to tell me that he had incorporated our suggestions into the letter, which he was about to mail to Cynthia. Rewriting the letter had been for him a moving experience, equal in intensity to the one the three of us had shared days earlier. He had found new levels of understanding as he reread the words of his revised letter. He had let go of a great deal of fear and frustration about the agreement as he began to focus on how empowering it would be for Cynthia to release him, and in doing so to release herself, from the bonds of the former relationship.

Being able to look at the situation without animosity, without venom, with an awareness of the love he still held for his former wife and of his own need for healing as well as hers, was a gift Gerry received with gratitude. In that moment, Gerry did not see Cynthia as an obstacle to his plans for a new lifestyle. He did not see her as the cause of the conflict he had been experiencing. Rather, he saw the light in him joined with the light in her. It is an experience anyone can have who chooses, even momentarily, to see beyond their attachment to outcomes.

In relating that story I do not mean to leave the impression that Gerry's becoming free to pursue with Brenda a spiritual lifestyle, and being released from his financial obligations to Cynthia and their children, was the *only* or the *preferred* outcome, from a spiritual perspective. Some readers may identify with Gerry's desires and dilemma; others may feel he acted irresponsibly and selfishly and did not honour his obligations. The point is that his opportunity for healing was not so much in *what* he did, but rather in how he did it. He had a range of choices to make, and an opportunity to find his peace in any and all of them. The fact that he was unable to find healing in the status quo does not mean that it was not there to find. For his own reasons he preferred to face other choices, and it was in respect of those choices that he was called upon to reach out to Cynthia in the incident I have related.

Gerry's legal relationship with Cynthia may present further opportunities for healing down the road. As much as I would like to report that Cynthia was transformed upon her receipt of Gerry's letter, and was overcome with the spirit of forgiveness, I cannot state that to be so. Although I have never met her, I believe she continues to harbour a lot of anger and resentment towards Gerry. However, that is not something either of them should feel guilty about. Nor is it to be taken as a "failure" of the healing process I have just described. As I mentioned earlier, stories of forgiveness, powerful attestations though they may be of the healing of the one who forgives, do not always have what we may think of as happy outcomes.

It is important to acknowledge, as well, that healing is a state of mind. As long as we are in the world we move in and out of that state. It is a constant vigil to maintain the state of mind, in the face of rejection, rebuff and temptation to give in to the conflict we feel in most of life's situations. To my mind, the important thing is not to focus on *when* healing is received; it is to affirm that at some point each one of us receives it. That point is determined by our own choices. In everything we do we are given the opportunity to open a window or a door to our own and someone else's healing. In choosing to accept the opportunity, healing comes. In choosing to reject it, healing is postponed.

It may also be that Cynthia can forgive Gerry and still ask that he honour the legal obligation she may consider he owes her. She can do this by choosing peace above whatever attachment she has in the outcome. In saying that, I acknowledge that it can be very difficult at times to choose peace above the outcomes we have pre-judged as our preferred ones. It requires trust, love and acceptance to choose the peace that healing brings, for it often comes in forms very different from what it was we thought we wanted.

What both Gerry and Cynthia, and indeed all those who find themselves entangled in legal disputes of one sort or another, can ask themselves is whether the law, and what they perceive to be their respective legal positions, is helping or hindering their recognition of their spiritual unity and the healing that comes from that recognition. Are they looking at law as something that is keeping them in a state of conflict, or as presenting them with an opportunity for healing their conflict?

In that regard, healing is never about winning, or realizing outcomes, or satisfying our egos' passion for justice. It is a sense of peace in the face of whatever seems to confront us. It is acceptance that we are not alone in the world, that our strength nourishes others, and theirs us; that our interests are those of others and theirs ours. Healing is overcoming the loneliness of separation by piercing the illusion of separateness and seeing ourselves in others. Law can keep healing from us, or it can prompt us to find it. We can find it if we are willing to look hard at the situations in which we are invited to use law and to recognize in them our fears, our grievances, our attachments and our judgment. It is in offering our minds the choice to forgive, to let go of the illusions that imprison us, that law earns the description "an opportunity for healing."

## CONFLICT

I want to acknowledge at the outset of this discussion that there are many aspects of law that do not seem, at least in the abstract, to raise a lot of conflict in people. Much of our law simply boils down to common sense. It formalizes rules of conduct with which most people would agree, if they stopped to think about the matter. Who would question that we should take reasonable care to avoid injuring other people? It makes sense that there should be laws to regulate driving on highways and carrying out safety checks on automobiles. Who can complain about laws that allow for compensation to be paid to workers who are injured on the job, or social assistance to the less fortunate? Surely, as well, there have to be rules governing the ownership and transfer of property, and to deal with its disposition when we pass on. These are all rules made up by people like you and me, except that their jobs are to think about such matters and to develop laws. Through experience and a process of refinement rules change and are adapted to new situations.

A lot of my days as a lawyer, and those of my colleagues, are spent simply helping to make the wheels of the world turn in a more or less even rhythm. There is a lot of planning, administration and detail to be taken care of as people strive to observe the rules that are laid down by society. We have made a somewhat complicated world in acting out our fearful belief in separateness, and there is a lot of room for the law's facilitating role.

The point at which conflict surfaces is when we start to feel that someone is out to "get us," to use the law to make our lives difficult. It may be a neighbour, a family member, a stranger, a city planner or the police. It may be the government, which we continuously accuse of strangling us with more and more costly red tape and regulation, or of adding increased weight to an already onerous tax burden.

Mostly we feel the conflict arising out of the *application* of the law as it hits us close to home and threatens our sense of security, our pocket books, our families, our sense of independence, and sometimes simply the value we place on our time. I recall a recent experience I had struggling to read and to understand a lengthy and complicated municipal sign by-law, which I had been asked to look into by a local church. I observed myself fuming at the complexity of a law to regulate what seemed to me to be a petty and unwarranted intrusion into the church's freedom to place whatever kind of sign it wanted on its property. In abject frustration I did what I should have done in the first place: simply call the person who administers the by-law. Within a few minutes the man with whom I spoke, who was both knowledgable and helpful, had cleared up my confusion (I had even been reading an out-dated version of the by-law) and had offered to send me the necessary papers. It was a good illustration to me of how we allow ourselves unnecessarily to be drawn toward conflict simply by the way in which we approach situations.

Many people would probably respond that I was fortunate to get hold of someone who was so helpful. How often have you heard stories about calls such as mine to government offices serving only to heighten the conflict? We are often quick to pin the responsibility for our conflict on the person at the other end of the line. But is that an accurate assessment of what is going on? Can we ever hold anyone other than ourselves responsible for how we react to any situation we face? How willing are we to acknowledge our eagerness to heap blame on someone else for what it is we think is bothering us?

Seeing law as an opportunity for healing is helped immeasurably by a willingness to look at "conflict" in a way that to some may seem unorthodox. I am attempting in this book to bring to litigation, to alternative dispute resolution (ADR), and indeed to all conflict resolution processes, a spiritual and psychological dimension of conflict that is largely absent from the discussion contained in contemporary studies and writing on these subjects. Most, if not all, of the current writing on conflict resolution is premised on two assumptions that are not part of my analysis: 1) that conflict is "real," in the sense that it has a source outside my mind; 2) that conflict resolution requires a solution that is either agreed to or imposed upon the parties who are "in conflict." My position is that conflict is illusory and that its resolution in the end is a *unilateral* process.

I invite readers to give consideration to the thought that "conflict" is not a situation, but rather a state of mind. It is true that we commonly speak of an individual as being "in conflict with the law," an idea which does have objective content in the sense that the person's behaviour is measured by the law and found wanting. In this context, "conflict resolution" means bringing the person around to the point that he or she conducts him/herself in accordance with the dictates of society, as proclaimed in the law. However, it is what underlies these behavioral manifestations that I am addressing as "conflict."

I see conflict as being a decision that I make about how I choose to experience what I think someone is doing to me or what I see myself as doing to someone else. I may see myself as a victim or as a victimizer, but in either case I am looking outside myself for someone to blame for the role I assume. I may be reacting to something someone is saying, or I may perceive my interests as being intruded upon by what someone is doing. In either case, I have given birth to the conflict by investing in the correctness of my perception that the cause of my upset lies outside of me, in someone or something else. From a spiritual/psychological perspective, I have invented the entire situation. I have given it all the meaning it has for me. I have created both the problem and what I regard as the solution, projected them outwardly, and then perceived them as "objective reality." I have convinced myself that the "conflict" is a situation "out there," forgetting that what I seem to be experiencing "out there" is but the reflection of what I am experiencing in my mind. Stripped to the core, the conflict I seem to be experiencing in the world is really the struggle that is continuously played out in my mind between that part of me that looks at the world from my ego vantage point (wrong mindedness), and that part that is attuned to the thought of unity and healing (right mindedness).

Other persons with whom I convince myself from time to time that I am in conflict, and indeed whom I may hold responsible for the conflict I am experiencing, usually look at the facts differently than I do, and experience their own conflict as stemming from something *I* did. They become attached to that different view, and blame *me* for threatening that attachment. And yet, when you analyze what is going on, both the conflict and its source are always internal to the one who experiences it; in that sense there is no "objective reality" to conflict. It is *always* a decision I make about my experiences, just as it is a decision you make about yours.

The resolution of my conflict is likewise internal. I can look at each seeming conflict as a "problem" or as an opportunity. If I choose to find peace within myself, there is no conflict. If I decide not to find peace within myself, then the conflict remains, no matter how I may manipulate the seeming outer trappings of my conflict in search of its solution.

I feel fortunate that I have not had many personal encounters with legal conflict. A few years ago, however, my son, Geoffrey, who was then an undergraduate at university, was involved in an automobile accident while driving one of my cars back to school. Because the car was old, I had removed the collision insurance. As a result, my insurance company would not accept any responsibility for helping me recover the value of the vehicle, which had been irreparably damaged in the accident. I was on my own to recover, if I could, from the other parties and their insurance company.

I remember distinctly my son telephoning me after the accident and introducing the subject by assuring me that "the other driver had been at fault." He told me he had been driving reasonably in his own lane when the other car, proceeding in the adjacent lane in the same direction ahead of him, had skidded on the ice out of control into his lane. Because of the adjacent traffic, and the short space available for braking, Geoffrey saw no alternative but to drive into the vehicle that was spread across his lane. He was certain that he had done all he could to stop his car, and felt quite proud that he had swerved to avoid hitting the front passenger door of the other vehicle. He had a vivid recollection of the frightened look on the face of the woman in the passenger seat, and felt that he had perhaps saved her life.

I called the couple in the other car the next day to verify insurance information. We had a pleasant, but guarded, conversation, and I had little doubt that the matter could be easily resolved in our favour. I obtained a police report which, though sketchy, appeared to confirm my son's explanation of the accident. It was with some upset, therefore, that I learned later from the insurer of the other vehicle that our claim was being denied. When I spoke to the adjuster, he advised me that his clients' version of the accident was significantly different from my son's, that he had concluded that my son was at fault, and that the company would not pay.

After sending off a few letters designed to intimidate[14] the other parties and their insurer, without any apparent success, I decided I would let the matter drop. The amount at stake was too little to warrant hiring a lawyer (because the accident had occurred in another province, I felt I could not handle it). My son was a little upset with me about this, as he had considered the car to be his, morally speaking, and he did not easily accept the idea of being without "his" car and without the means to purchase a replacement. I told him that if he could recover the money, it would be his. With that, he decided he would pursue the matter in Small Claims Court, which would not allow him to recover the full value of the vehicle but would leave him farther ahead than he would be if he hired a lawyer to bring the suit in a higher court.

---

[14]     Evidently, I was not in those moments seeing the incident "differently." One must be vigilant against the temptation of old "habits." My recounting of the story is a part of that vigilance.

Having filed the necessary papers (at the last moment and with some help from me, I should add), my son waited for his trial. Finally, he received notice of the trial date, and he began to prepare his case. As might be expected, he consulted me from time to time for advice. I impressed upon him the importance of staying calm and reassured, and of restating the facts as he remembered them, as objectively and as dispassionately as possible. I cautioned him to expect a different version of the accident from the other parties, but not to be flustered or to react in either an aggressive or a defensive way. I told him that the judge would decide on the basis of the facts as he saw them presented in evidence, and that he had to accept that. If he became attached to the outcome, he was going to have a bad experience, win or lose.

After the trial, my son related to me his experience. He had more or less followed my advice, although his case had been at the very end of the day's docket and had been disposed of in a hurry. For that reason, he felt that he had not developed his case as fully as he would have liked. Nonetheless, he thought he had made his essential points. He reported that he had gone out of his way to be pleasant to the other parties, and not to speak in any way disparagingly of them. He had the clear impression, however, that the other parties were openly hostile towards him and his friend, who had been his witness, and were extremely upset at having been dragged into court over this matter. He sensed that hostility pervading the legal defence the representative of the insurance company made to his claim.

A few weeks later the judgment was issued, and Geoffrey had won his case. He felt extremely pleased, and even more so when the cheque arrived from the insurance company a few days later.  My point is not that he won because of the attitude he displayed in presenting his case, although that may well have been a factor in his success.  What is important is that, in the process leading up to the result, he had acquired, I think, some sense that he was responsible for the conflict he felt and how he dealt with it.  He did not require any form of overt reconciliation with the other side in order to find his peace.

At the same time, I think it is fair to observe that if he had truly found his peace within himself he would not have continued to focus as he did on the upset and hostility he felt he was picking up from the other side.  Their conflict was a mirror of unresolved thoughts within his own mind, and in that sense his forgiveness was not as complete as either he or I might like to imagine.  But at least his experience was a beginning. In his willingness to look at his own reactions and to refrain from feeding off what he saw in his "adversaries" in order to justify an attack on them, he demonstrated a willingness to see differently.  In time he may come to understand that their apparent hostility to him had really nothing to do with him, personally, but was a projection of the fear, guilt and anger they felt within themselves.  In an ultimate sense, it was what *A Course in Miracles* refers to as "a call for love,"[15] an expression of our deep discomfort with our belief in separation. It is our willingness to respond to that call *with* love, rather than to react with anger, that resolves the conflict we experience in our minds.

If my goal is peace (and that is the most important choice

---

[15]   See e.g. Text, p. 202, where fear and attack are both seen as a call for love, to be answered by giving love to the one who calls for it.

I make), then using the legal process to *reinforce* my attachment to the correctness of my legal position will not achieve my goal. I will remain in a state of conflict. To resolve the conflict, I have to find another way. As I have tried to point out with the example of my son, this does not necessarily mean abandoning the use of law and the legal system and simply capitulating to the position to which my perceived adversary is attached. Rather, it involves looking at what the situation brings up for me, seeing the legal process differently, replacing attack thoughts with forgiveness and finding peace, whatever the outcome.

The key, I am convinced, is how one *uses* the legal process. Even litigation may become a tool for true conflict resolution, i.e. a tool used for resolving the conflict in my mind, if I am coming from the right place in using it. As radical as it may seem, consider the following hypothetical model:

1) The litigant acknowledges that the conflict is in his own mind, and that it is a creation of his own mind.

2) The litigant recognizes that his stake in the outcome of the process (i.e. in having his view of the situation upheld by the court) is causing him a lot of upset and anxiety.

3) The litigant abandons his sense of vulnerability, and determines to trust in the process. This is very much a matter of faith and acceptance.

4) The litigant continuously forgives his "adversary."

Approached in this way, legal process is used as an aid

to healing. It is not that the litigation *resolves* the conflict; rather, it provides a process and environment in which conflict resolution can occur in me. Resolving the conflict is not dependent upon the other litigant approaching the litigation in the same way, as was evident in the ostensibly hostile approach taken by my son's "adversaries." However, the fact that one litigant approaches the situation in this way, and responds to the other without the anger and blame that so often dominates the process, may well assist in healing the conflict experienced by the other. Implicit in the approach is the tacit invitation to the other to join in the healing process.[16]

Litigation is only one process in which this discipline can be applied for resolving conflict. It works equally in arbitration and other adjudicative processes. It also applies, perhaps more comfortably, to mediation, where the expectation is that the parties will themselves, with the help of a third party, reach an agreement on the issues, rather than assign a decision making role to a third party. I do not mean to suggest that it is *easy* for us to give up our stake in our preferred outcomes of any of these processes, and to simply trust that the process will come up with an appropriate result. But it is in looking at and recognizing how our attachments consume us, and in finding our willingness to release judgment, that healing can occur. When we are fully in that state, the formal outcome of the process becomes a secondary consideration.

---

[16] It is often the willingness of the litigant and of his or her lawyer to work together toward the goal of healing that determines whether the process will help or hinder the resolution of conflict. This relationship will be explored in greater depth later in this book, in Part III, Functions.

These ideas can also be applied to the conflict that is experienced in the criminal justice system, as difficult as it may seem to look at many of these situations in terms of choices. People can perceive themselves as being victimized by the controlling forces of society; or they can see their situations as an opportunity to release attachments, to forgive and to heal. And just as the healing of individual minds requires looking at our attachments to ideas about preferred outcomes, the healing of our societies requires that we look at our individual and collective moral indignation towards offenders, at our self-righteousness, and at our fear that forgiveness will lead to anarchy. We would benefit greatly as individuals and as a society if we could find within ourselves the willingness to look at criminal justice as something other than attack, control and vengeance. In accepting that responsibility for ourselves we help others to see their own choices, and, in particular, to see the opportunity that each situation offers for healing.

The starting point is with each one of us. How we think and feel as individuals affects social consciousness. If I am in conflict, I live in a conflicted world. If I am at peace, I live without conflict, because I see the world in a different light. It is open to each of us to see in law, and in the legal system, either oppression and conflict, or an opportunity for forgiveness and healing. In making our own choices for healing we open doors for others to make similar choices.

I entertain no illusions that everyone is committed to peace, healing and true conflict resolution. Our culture is heavily steeped in conflict, judgment and control, and for many people the ideas expressed in this book will have no immediate attraction. I believe, however, that there are those who *are* ready and willing to look beyond judgment and control for ways of truly healing conflict. For them, the legal system is an untapped resource, presenting unlimited opportunities to practice forgiveness of others, resulting in self-forgiveness and ultimately in the healing of ourselves, our neighbours and our society.

# PART II - JUDGMENT

Be innocent of judgment, unaware of any thoughts of evil or of good that ever crossed your mind of anyone. Now do you know him not. But you are free to learn of him, and learn of him anew. Now is he born again to you, and you are born again to him, without the past that sentenced him to die, and you with him. Now is he free to live as you are free, because an ancient learning passed away, and left a place for truth to be reborn.

*A Course in Miracles*, Text, page 603.

## RIGHTS

The choice for healing is often made more difficult by the law's preoccupation with "rights." We have a strong attachment to our rights. We are taught that our rights are our badges of individuality, the foundation of our separate interests, and our means of self-identification and self-fulfilment.

When we focus on our "rights," it is easy to think about our interests as being separate from those of others, and to think that someone else may be taking away what is "ours." If someone seems to intrude on our rights, we have a tendency to judge. We may emphasize loss and think of ourselves as being attacked. If so, we may feel inclined to attack back, failing to recognize that, in attacking others, we attack ourselves and deny ourselves the peace that comes with healing.

How many stories have been told, particularly in relation to family disputes, about potentially amicable settlements being sabotaged once lawyers became involved? Friends, families, co-workers, and even strangers reinforce our fears that we are going to be "taken" by another person. And so we want to know what our "rights" are. Once we have been told, we have great difficulty looking at those rights in anything but a separated mind frame. To accept less than our rights may be seen as weakness; to be denied our rights leaves us victimized. Can rights be seen any other way? Are they necessarily instruments for judging, attacking and controlling others?

I do not mean to suggest that we should not know what our rights are. It's just that we have to be attentive to what that knowledge brings up for us. I accept that it can be helpful to know what our rights are. Rights can serve as benchmarks, as a way of looking at situations differently, as a way of releasing ideas that block the healing of conflict in our minds. It may well be, for example, that knowing my legal rights will lead me to realize and to accept that the position I am holding on to is excessive, unrealistic and beyond reasonable expectations. Conversely, to be informed that my expectations are significantly lower than the law allows may help me to achieve higher levels of self-realization and a better sense of my worth. My current expectations may have been devalued by low self-esteem and by cultural conditioning. That is not to suggest that we should or can look to the law as the *source* of or definition of our worth, but it may jolt us into a process of re-evaluation.

Just because I am informed about my rights does not mean that I must use them to attack others. It is when I insist upon my rights as a means of judging others, or of hurting others, or when I feel guilty about "compromising" my rights, or I feel victimized in accepting what is less than my due, that my attachment to rights gets in the way of healing. Many people experience those kinds of feelings when they are caught up in the legal system. They expect their lawyers to "fight" for their rights; they accept less than "their due" only with bitterness; and they emerge scarred. It is not difficult to understand why the pursuit and defence of rights leads many people to experience such a strong sense of separation and conflict.

There is a popular expression, "would you rather be right than happy?"[17] It is a kind of antidote to the stress that one can experience when rights are in issue. Insisting on having

---

[17] It is expressed in *A Course in Miracles* at page 573 of the Text as: "Do you prefer to be right or happy?" It is a reminder that our happiness is never found outside ourselves.

our rights is almost always a sure path to unhappiness. Attachment to our rights can imprison us. That is not to say that we *cannot* enjoy the benefits of our rights along with our happiness. It is just that we cannot have both while we are in a state of conflict; coming to grips with our attachment to being right is a prerequisite to healing conflict, and ultimately to enjoying our rights.

A way of looking at rights differently is to ask whether, in upholding them, we are giving *to* or taking *from* the person with whom we are in dispute. When I claim my rights, do I maintain a loving perspective? Am I genuinely offering an opportunity for healing to the other person, or am I trying to make him or her a loser? In what ways will the interests of others be enhanced by the result I seek? Can I see good in this for everyone concerned? Am I placing the highest good of everyone above my personal attachment to upholding my rights?[18] To see this universal benefit requires a vigilant attitude against the fear, guilt and control that continuously tempt me to seek refuge, not healing, in my "rights."[19]

Looking at rights as being about more than self-interest is perhaps easier with egalitarian rights than with legal rights.

---

[18]  This idea is expressed in Lesson 77 of *A Course in Miracles*, "I am entitled to miracles." The lesson includes the reminder that "miracles are never taken from one and given to another, and that in asking for your rights, you are upholding the rights of everyone."

[19]  *A Course in Miracles*, in the Manual for Teachers, p. 3, describes a "teacher of God" as anyone who "has made a deliberate choice in which he did not see his interests as apart from someone else's."

Egalitarian rights express the principle that we are all equal under and before the law. The law frowns on discrimination, and prescribes several ways in which discriminatory behaviour can be called into account. In Canada, the *Canadian Charter of Rights and Freedoms* and the *Canadian Bill of Rights*, as well as various federal and provincial human rights statutes, present the idea of equality, of oneness, of spiritual unity and brotherhood. Similar concepts are expressed in the *Bill of Rights* of the United States Constitution, and in human rights legislation at both the federal and state levels. These laws are strong forces in support of healing, both for communities and for individuals. If we could truly honour this teaching, and integrate it into our experiences, we would be enriched as communities and as individuals. These laws speak universal truth.

At the point of their enforcement, however, it is easy to lose sight of the spiritual principles underlying these laws. It is easy to fall into the trap of characterizing the players in human rights dramas as victims and victimizers. There can be a strong temptation to project anger, resentment, fear and guilt onto others, thus fuelling the conflict we experience, whether as players in the drama or as observers. There may be a sense of group separation. An entire class may be seen as victimized, and the members of the class who are upholding its rights may see the class, as well as themselves, as victims of the oppressive forces of mainstream society. The focus can rest upon identifying winners and losers. The mood can shift to one of attack and defence, notwithstanding that mechanisms for mediation and reconciliation are often built into the processes that have been designed to enforce these laws. Within such a climate, any thought of spiritual unity can deteriorate into "tolerance" and "compromise," which are attitudes of mind that are not conducive to the healing of conflict. I think of "tolerance" as the *repression* of anger and hostility, not the expression of love and forgiveness. And, for me, "compromise" signifies only a *conditional* relinquishment of our attachments, not an unconditional shift in attitude. Both entail pragmatic gestures that seek to control and manage, not to heal, the inner conflict that is experienced when we lose sight of our spiritual unity.

I find it helpful to remember that spiritual unity does not mean uniformity. Uniqueness in the world of form does not seem frightening if I can view it simply as the way each of us has chosen to express his or her experience of spiritual unity. In recognizing my neighbour's egalitarian rights, I respect and reinforce his or her experience and expression of spiritual unity. It is the belief in *my separateness* that engenders the fear that drives me to seek refuge in uniformity, and to resist my neighbour's right to expression. Recognizing our spiritual unity leads me to *celebrate* my neighbour's uniqueness, not to denigrate and destroy it in my fearful quest for uniformity.

This illustrates the fundamental choice we have: we can use our "rights" in the cause of healing, or we can use them to judge and attack. Rights reinforce healing whenever they are used to facilitate the expression of our spiritual unity in the infinite ways, each unique, that spiritual unity can be expressed in form. However, they retard healing when we seek to protect and enforce our rights in a state of fear, rather than in a state of love. We reject our spiritual unity, we affirm our belief that we are separate, and we find ourselves in conflict.

To be asked to look at rights essentially as means of

affirming our unity with our neighbours and with God, rather than advancing our own self-interest, may seem threatening to many, and may raise a lot of fearful thoughts. I want to emphasize, however, that to choose healing does not imply sacrifice. It does not mean that I must submit to whatever demands someone makes of me or my property, however hurtful to me or to others this may seem to be. After all, to learn from our relationships in the world requires that we participate in what the world offers. Pursuing a spiritual path is not made easier by allowing ourselves to become dysfunctional in the world. What it requires is that we commit ourselves to looking at what is really going on whenever we find ourselves taking refuge in our rights. Are we experiencing peace or conflict? Are we *attacking* our neighbours as we address our relationships within a legal framework, or can we still honour them as children of God while using the law to help settle our differences?

Healing is rising above the *forms* into which our attachments to our rights tend to draw us, and seeing the underlying *content* that is expressed in the thought that love, not fear, is real. Our rights do not help us to see what is real when we use them to reinforce and react to our fears. Healing requires that we relinquish all judgment that is implicit in the reliance we place on our rights; it requires that we see our rights as benefiting everyone, or no one. That is the challenge of seeing rights differently.

## OBLIGATIONS

Legal obligations are the flip side of rights. Mary Ann Glendon of Harvard Law School, in her book *Rights Talk*,[20] has observed that the language of the law tends to be less focused on obligations and responsibilities than it is on rights.

By and large, my legal duty or obligation is to do that which is consistent with someone else's rights, or that which the government has determined to be in the public interest. For example, I have a duty not to do what a reasonable person could foresee might injure a neighbour. I have a duty to carry out my end of a legal contract into which I have entered. I have a legal obligation to repay money I have borrowed from a financial institution, and to pay my taxes.

The law tends to value legal obligations mostly in terms of money, although in those instances where money cannot be a sufficient basis for compensation, it allows for ways of compelling an obligation to be performed according to its specific terms. In the main, however, the law looks at the resolution of issues surrounding the fulfilment of obligations as being about money.

Obligations have great potential for engendering conflict. This stems from our fear of loss and lack, and our readiness to perceive almost anything as an attack. If I do not carry out my legal duty to someone else, chances are that person will feel attacked, and will want to attack me back to protect what is rightfully theirs.

---

[20] Mary Ann Glendon, *Rights Talk : the impoverishment of political discourse* (New York 1991).

This seems to be especially so when it involves money. Undoubtedly my bank would get nervous about the repayment of my loan if I were to miss a monthly payment. At the same time, I would likely become defensive, fearing that the bank would soon be on the attack if I didn't make my payment. The fear on both sides would escalate. The bank might seize and sell my house to avoid a loss, regardless of my personal circumstances. After all, business is business. Besides, how could the bank justify to others what would understandably be perceived as special treatment to me if my mortgage debt were waived? It would create a troublesome precedent, to say the least.

Fear manifests in judgment. The bank would begin to look at me as uncreditworthy, as financially irresponsible, as someone who defaults on loans. I would begin to look at the bank as harsh and oppressive, and I might even try to shift the blame onto the bank's shoulders for enticing me to borrow the money in the first place.

We can easily become conditioned to *fear* our obligations, rather than to *honour* them as ways of participating in the celebration of our experience of spiritual unity. If I do not feel separated from my neighbours, but rather I share the experience of unity with them, then I can appreciate that the fulfilment of my obligations is really of benefit to myself as well as to my neighbours. If I can forgive what I may perceive to be sharp practices by my neighbours, and instead focus on the fulfilment of *my* obligations to them, treating it as an opportunity to heal what may be conflicted feelings I have towards them, then the experience can be a healing one. In many situations, of course, I may see my obligations as being conditional on my neighbours fulfilling theirs, and there may be disagreement about the nature and extent of the obligations each of us undertook. My ability to see peace in these situations is enhanced by the discipline outlined elsewhere in this book for approaching litigation and other dispute resolution processes. Essentially, I have to look at and move beyond my attachment to the correctness of my perception of what my obligations, as well as those of my neighbour, are in each situation. I must also release my fear of *lack*, which maintains my focus on the monetary implications my obligations have for me, and away from the idea of service to the community of which I am a part.

To be at peace with our *obligations* is not a goal that is any more easily accomplished than to see our *rights* in terms of the interests of all. It is, I believe, most easily attained within the philosophical framework of spiritual unity. If we can look at our own obligations, and those of others, through forgiving eyes, judgment evaporates and their fulfilment can be a healing experience.

## FAULT

In law, my rights are often conditional on someone else's state of blameworthiness. For example, my contractual rights are enforceable when the other party is in *breach*. My right to recover damages for personal injury usually arises only where someone has *intentionally* or *negligently* injured me. To assert my rights, I often have to point my finger at someone else.

In criminal law, the focus is on what is called the *mens rea* of the accused. This is the blameworthy state of mind. The law uses words such as the "accused," the "defendant," and the "offender," to describe the alleged "guilty" person.

These concepts, and the language in which they are expressed, cannot but help reinforce the sense of "victim" that is experienced by the person whose rights were violated. It must be very difficult to love and forgive the person the prosecutor has had you point your finger at in order to obtain a conviction, or against whom you have had to testify in order to prove civil liability. I am grateful that I have not yet personally had to face either situation.

Not all areas of the law are preoccupied with fault. There are laws, for example those relating to wills, estates, trusts and property, that regulate human affairs and dealings simply by prescribing the ways in which certain things are to be done. As well, with the advent of no-fault automobile insurance, the law has abandoned the link between compensation and fault with respect to certain kinds of traffic accidents and injuries. In addition, the concept of "strict liability," which is applied in relation to the use of dangerous items, and in some countries to compensate for injuries caused by defective manufactured products, has largely eliminated the element of fault in assessing civil liability for those kinds of injuries. In any of those categories, however, circumstances can arise in which the focus of the parties is on fault, even though it may not be a required element of legal liability.

I believe it is possible to see any situation differently, if I am committed to healing. The key is to translate in my mind the notion of "fault" into that of "error." Anyone can make a mistake. We all do. However, it is easier to forgive what we believe to be a mistake than it is to forgive what we believe to be a "sin." I may want to be *compensated* for what someone else's mistake has cost me, but this does not mean that I must treat it as a question of moral blame.

To train the mind to make that translation requires overcoming significant resistance. The legal concept of "fault" is a reflection of our strong personal and societal attachment to moral values. It underscores our inclination to look outside ourselves to someone else as the source of our perceived problems, and to focus on our interests and rights as being distinct from those of others. My preoccupation with finding fault in others conveniently masks the fact that I have projected my own sense of deficiency and guilt out onto other people. I am sure that everyone can identify times when their seeming anger towards another person was really a redirection of the anger felt towards themselves for placing themselves in a particular situation.

Because it underscores "fault," the law can be seen as a significant obstacle to my locating and resolving within *me* the conflict I associate with my "problem." Nonetheless, it seems to me that if, on analysis, I am resorting to the legal system to establish someone else's fault as a means of unburdening myself of my own guilt and anger, I am choosing a very difficult and expensive way of doing it, and a way that cannot succeed. I cannot achieve self-forgiveness by casting blame on someone else. It is totally inconsistent with the principle of spiritual unity discussed earlier in the context of healing. I cannot help but wonder, when I look at situations in that light, how many of the billions of dollars spent each year in legal costs are being spent on what is essentially a misdirected search for self-forgiveness. If we could see our attraction to law in that way, we might come to the realization that there are much easier, much cheaper and more successful ways of healing our conflict.

That having been said, the important thing is to choose a way to deal with conflict in whatever situation we may find ourselves, whether it be in a family discussion or in a protracted courtroom battle. The form in which the conflict arises does not really matter; an opportunity presents itself in each situation to approach healing in essentially the same way. I can heal conflict only by keeping at the front of my mind the thought of spiritual unity. To give practical content to that thought in a legal context, I can remind myself that the law's function is not to force or even to invite me to make value judgments about my neighbour. To the extent that the law and my use of it expresses values, those values can reflect love and healing, rather than fear and guilt. I have control over what the law means to me personally, and what I choose to use it for. Whether I am a lawyer, a judge, a legislator or a private citizen, I can take responsibility for my own use of law and legal process. I can ask myself whether I am coming from a loving or a fearful place, whether I am committed to inner healing, or to conflict and judgment. I have the choice to see someone's "fault" as moral blameworthiness, or as a mistake that can be corrected.

As long as I choose to see the law and the legal system as a play about fault, it will only strengthen my commitment to judging, attacking and controlling others. To look at law differently is to open to the possibility that no matter what test the law may impose as the standard of liability, be it civil or criminal, it neither requires, nor warrants, my judgment. This theme will be explored further under the headings that follow.

## GUILT - INNOCENCE

"Monsieur the curé," said the man, "you are good; you do not despise me. You receive me into your house. You light your candles for me. Yet I have not hidden from you whence I come, and that I am an unfortunate man."

The Bishop, who was seated by his side, gently touched his hand. "You need not have told me who you were. This is not my house; it is the house of Christ. This door does not ask a man who enters whether he has a name, but if he has a sorrow. You suffer, you are hungry and thirsty; you are welcome. Do not thank me, or say that I am receiving you in my house, for no one is at home here except the man who needs refuge. I tell you, who are a passer-by, that you are more at home here than I am myself; everything here is yours. What need have I to know your name? Besides, before you told me, you had one which I knew."

The man opened his eyes in amazement.

"Is that true? You knew my name?"

"Yes," replied the Bishop, "you are my brother."

Victor Hugo, *Les Miserables*

Closely related to the concept of fault is that of "guilt," offset by the corresponding concept of "innocence." These are terms used in criminal law to reflect the idea of moral blameworthiness, which underlies criminal liability for most offences.

There is no denying that people do things that have

terrifying implications for others. The newspapers are filled each day with stories of murder, rape, sexual abuse, reckless driving, robbery, fraud and on and on. It is both easy and natural for us to fall into judgment of those "offenders." The stories bring to the surface our deepest fears, and our empathy and compassion go out to the "victims," their families and friends. There is a strong urge in all of us to hold someone "guilty" for what has transpired. We project our emotions onto the offenders, and we judge. And while we are in judgment, we are not at peace.

I read recently in the newspaper the shocking story of a three year old girl who had been sexually assaulted and murdered. It was the manifestation of every parent's nightmare. The parents reacted by calling for the return of the death penalty for child-killers. They were reported to have said that their hurt would not begin to heal until the offender had been caught and, presumably, convicted and punished. I found it was very easy, at least in that moment, to empathize with those strong emotions, even though it goes directly against the central message of my writing - i.e. that we receive healing through forgiveness. The incident illustrates the difficult emotional barriers we have to overcome in order to find our peace in the world. There are so many things that seem to happen that attract us towards expressing vengeance that to invite forgiveness may seem at times beyond our capability.

Although I taught criminal law for many years, I have had only limited exposure to it as a practicing lawyer. I do recall, however, the gripping experience of my first major criminal trial as a young lawyer. I was junior counsel defending a man who was accused of murdering his common-law wife by choking her and then drowning her in a bathtub. As horrendous as the crime seemed, the circumstances added a human dimension to the tragic result. The man had returned home after drinking excessively. The woman, in an upset state, had made some insulting remarks towards the man. In a state of rage, he grabbed her by the throat and choked her until she passed out. In what seemed to be an effort to revive her, he placed her in the bathtub, and turned on the faucets. Unable to revive her, it seems that in a state of panic he left her there. Her body slipped under the water and she died of asphyxiation by drowning. Within hours, upon sobering up and realizing the seriousness of the situation, the man turned himself over to the police.

The man had no previous record, and no apparent history of violent conduct. When I met him I was amazed at how such a quiet and unassuming man could be in such a terrible mess. Standing before me, I thought, was the murderer in all of us. In many ways, he seemed to be the victim of bizarre circumstances that he undoubtedly had had control over, but whose outcome he had never remotely foreseen. Love had turned to rage. And although, in the moment, he may have felt that rage more intensely than I would ever admit of myself, I have no doubt it was the same rage that I have felt at times. *A Course in Miracles* reminds us that there is no difference between a small upset and an intense fury.[21] It is all an attack on our neighbours, on ourselves and on God. We must not be too quick to judge another person simply because the outward manifestations of the attack appear to be more serious in one

---

[21] *A Course in Miracles*, in Lesson 21 at page 32 of the Workbook, reminds us that "a slight twinge of annoyance is nothing but a veil drawn over intense fury."

case than in another.

I believed then, and still believe, that we are all capable of criminal actions. And we must each accept responsibility for the choices we make that lead us to the fulfilment of that capability. However, it is not my role to judge others by attributing their behaviour to a sinful and evil nature. That is not to say that I cannot be part of a process to determine whether or not someone has transgressed the laws of the world and must receive the penalty that the law prescribes. But, in making that determination, I can attribute the person's behaviour to a fundamental mistake in their way of thinking and looking at themselves and others, an outgrowth of their belief that we are separate from each other. Otherwise, I deny that person's innocence as a component of our spiritual unity.

Although I did not, at the time, appreciate it quite in those terms, I think I understood that my role was to forgive, not to judge, this man for what he seemed to have done. I believe now that there was no other basis upon which I could have served him as a lawyer. And there was no other basis upon which I could have healed the conflict in my mind that arose when I first looked at the tragic circumstances this case presented.

Our client, although charged with murder, was convicted of the lesser offence of manslaughter. The judge gave the man the maximum sentence for the offence, twelve years, which was an unusually high sentence for manslaughter. I think the sentence reflected a strong moral judgment the judge had formed during the trial about the blameworthiness of the accused for the woman's death. Our client was released on parole after serving several years in prison. He had been a model prisoner, had acquired a trade and, as far as I am aware, resumed a relatively normal life.

Sometime later I represented a man who, a number of years earlier, had been acquitted on grounds of insanity of a charge of brutally stabbing a young girl in a department store. He had been committed indefinitely to a mental institution, and was then seeking release. The psychiatric opinion was that he was a sociopath and not an appropriate candidate for release, either then or for a considerable period of time in the future.

I was astounded to meet a very likeable and intelligent young man, and I quickly formed the impression that, however grotesque the act he had committed may have been, he had now become the victim of a judgment-filled process, both legal and psychiatric, that was blocking a fair review of his status. I became particularly judgmental of the doctors, whom I saw as being unreasonably reluctant to assist in the release of my client, or, alternatively, his transfer to another system in which he could be independently reviewed. Looking back on the situation, it is clear to me that I had acquired a stake in the outcome that was creating in me a lot of conflict.

Eventually, some time after I had retired from the case, the cumulative efforts of a long line of lawyers (both before and after me) bore fruit, and the man was transferred to another province for observation and treatment. Some time later he was released from confinement on a conditional basis. After several months of leading a seemingly normal life he committed two sexual offences for which he was convicted and imprisoned. When I heard about this I had a strong urge to judge my former client, not only for the offences, but for "conning" me. I also had a strong urge to judge myself for whatever contribution I may have made towards securing his release, which had resulted in harm to others. I realize now that there was no basis at all for judgment in this situation. Mistakes were made by many people along the course of this man's life. Judging those who made them would do nothing to correct them, nor to heal the conflicted feelings felt by the many whose lives had been touched by this man over the years.

Despite the heinous appearance of the "crimes" committed by the two men in the stories I have just related, I have come to accept how important it is for me personally to relinquish any thoughts of moral blameworthiness I might be tempted to direct towards them. To think in terms of guilt and innocence, apart from the technical requirements of the criminal law, is to hold them apart from me. In my heart I know each of them was and is innocent, however tragic the choices they made along the way.[22] I do not pretend to understand their actions or why they occurred. What passes for truth, I know is illusion. My temptation to see guilt reflects my own fears and anxieties, which I must look at and release.

Our struggle with guilt and innocence, both as individuals and as a society, is highlighted in several recent discoveries that persons who had been found guilty of serious crimes were really innocent, not only in the spiritual sense but in terms of the legal system's understanding of guilt and innocence. These cases serve as reminders that the knowledge we have of any situation we seek to judge is limited. Judgment is not only an impediment to healing; it can result in mistakes

---

[22] As mentioned earlier, healing proceeds from the acceptance that everything we do can be seen as either the extension of love or a call for love.

about guilt and innocence within our legal system.

The most famous case in Canada in recent years is that of Donald Marshall, a Micmac Indian who was convicted in 1971, while still a youth, of killing another youth during an encounter in a park in Sydney, Nova Scotia. Marshall served over eleven years in prison before questions about his guilt began to be taken seriously. He was released on parole pending the results of a renewed investigation into the circumstances surrounding the offence, which eventually saw the person who had actually killed the youth convicted. Marshall was ultimately acquitted and compensated for his wrongful incarceration. It is a case that has raised much bitterness and acrimony, particularly in view of the racial discrimination that seems to have been directed towards Marshall throughout the sequence of events.

Another case that has made world headlines is that of the "Birmingham Six," six Irishmen who were convicted in 1974 of bombing two English pubs in an incident that killed twenty-one persons and left 162 injured. The persistence of a member of the opposition Labour Party, among others, led to an official inquiry, which revealed numerous abuses in the investigation of the offences of which the six men were convicted, including police brutality, perjury, forced confessions and coverup of evidence. The men were released in 1991 after serving almost seventeen years in prison. The inference to be drawn from the inquiry is that there may be many others in British prisons who have been convicted and sentenced for crimes they did not commit.

There appears to be growing support for the belief that similar fates have been suffered by two Ontario men, Rick Sauvé and Gary Comeau, who have served thirteen years in prison after being convicted of the shooting death of a man in a Port Hope, Ontario bar in 1978. Despite the fact that another man had confessed to the shooting in front of the jury, and despite appeal motions to the Ontario Court of Appeal and to the Supreme Court of Canada, the two men, who have always maintained their innocence, remain incarcerated.

The latest controversy surrounds David Milgaard, who has served over 22 years in prison for a murder in Saskatchewan he says he did not commit. His lawyer has presented evidence and representations to show that he was convicted on the basis of tenuous evidence, and to support allegations of a police coverup of subsequent facts that substantiate his persistent claim of innocence. After long and arduous efforts by Milgaard's mother, friends and lawyers, the Minister of Justice, in November 1991, referred the case to the Supreme Court of Canada to determine whether Milgaard is "the victim of a miscarriage of justice."

Certain facts surrounding another case in British Columbia have been brought to my personal attention. I have no doubt that there are many such cases that have never been reported in the press. Many informed commentators are now echoing the recommendation of the Royal Commission that inquired into Donald Marshall's case, that there should be an independent board established to consider and recommend as to the reference and disposition of claims of wrongful conviction, rather than having this done, as it presently is in Canada, by the federal Minister of Justice.

These cases illustrate that, in spite of its tradition of extending the benefit of reasonable doubt to those who are accused of crimes, the criminal justice system is capable of making mistakes about guilt and innocence. More often than not, we think of these mistakes as resulting in "guilty" persons being set free for want of certainty about their guilt. The tolerance we exhibit towards those "mistakes" can perhaps be explained in terms of our lack of total trust in the judgment others exhibit when making decisions about guilt and innocence in criminal proceedings. There is probably also a strong element of fear in each of us that we might find ourselves in situations in which our own innocence might not be recognized, but for the grace of "reasonable doubt."

The cases I have highlighted remind us that the concept of reasonable doubt is not always enough to offset the judgment that attends the administration of the criminal justice system. That is not to say that to slip into judgment is not perfectly understandable. It is easy to see how a pressing desire to find someone to blame for a tragic occurrence can lead people to project their feelings of fear and anger onto the most likely suspect. The pressure to "solve" crimes, and to satisfy the community's passion for revenge and the need it senses for security, may seem overwhelming, and mistakes are made.

Nonetheless, documented cases of mistakes made in the administration of criminal justice demonstrate how important it is to look honestly at how deeply seated our attraction to judgment can be, and to work towards administering criminal justice without anger and vengeance. Guilt and innocence are likely to remain dominant concepts in the criminal law for some time; as tests for applying the rules of behaviour that society lays down, they may well be as useful as any. Still, these tests do not have to be administered in a way that denies our spiritual unity and the healing that flows from the thought of unity. The process the law prescribes for determining guilt and innocence can be carried out in a more loving and compassionate way. As difficult as it may seem to choose love and compassion in the face of the heinous crimes we read about daily in the newspapers, it is important to look at, and to recognize, how our anger and desire for vengeance not only block the experience of true justice, but bar the door to the healing that flows from it.

People who act out of fear and guilt can do what seem to be horrible things. Fortunately, we do not all respond to our fear and guilt in such destructive ways. Nevertheless, the attraction is there in all of us. It is too easy to justify the seemingly less destructive manifestations of our own fear and guilt by pointing out the terrible things other people do. Rather, we can be grateful for our willingness to listen to our inner guidance, and not be judgmental of those who seem unwilling or unable to listen to theirs. We all make choices, some with more harmful consequences than others, and it is *our* choices we must focus on, not those of another. The choices are always the same, in every situation: to follow the path of love or the path of fear. Those choices are present whenever we are tempted to judge another.

Even those who are locked up in prisons, condemned by juries as being guilty of heinous crimes, are children of God and carry their spiritual innocence with them. Some come into touch with that innocence, responding to the catalyst that their experience represents. Others do not. For each of them, society's condemnation for their crimes presents an opportunity for healing. Every circumstance in life gives forth the same opportunity. As they learn to forgive those whom they blame for their circumstances, and as we learn to forgive them for the crimes of which society has found them guilty, there is a recognition of the innocence we all share, and a healing of the guilt that imprisons us all in the world.

## JUSTICE

The law's emphasis on rights, fault and guilt is tied to its pursuit of *justice*. Everyone wants to see justice done, and looks to the law and to the legal system to deliver it. How many times have we heard the expressions: "Justice was done;" "justice was not done;" or so and so "was brought to justice." We seek to eliminate "unjust" laws or aspects of the system that allow for "injustice." We try to reform our laws to achieve better justice. We speak about "access" to justice through a better system of justice administration and more availability of information relevant to the justice system.

The concept of justice has a strong presence in the language of the law. There are Departments of Justice in governments, even of some countries the legal and political regimes of which we do not readily associate with our concept of "justice." We have a Minister of Justice in the Canadian federal government, and in the governments of all the provinces. We call most of our federally appointed judges "Justices." The *Canadian Charter of Rights and Freedoms* speaks of the "principles of fundamental justice." These words have been interpreted by the Supreme Court of Canada to embrace the presumptions of the common law and the expressions within international conventions on human rights that "have been recognized as essential elements of a system for the administration of justice which is founded upon a belief in 'the dignity and worth of the human person' (preamble to the *Canadian Bill of Rights...*) and on 'the rule of law' (preamble to the *Canadian Charter of Rights and Freedoms...).*"[23] [Note the absence of any reference to the "supremacy of God," a phrase which is also included in the preamble to the *Charter.*] The Court went on to state that the principles of fundamental justice "are to be found in the basic tenets of our legal system. They do not lie in the realm of general public policy but in the inherent domain of the judiciary as guardian of the justice system."[24]

The treatment of justice in legal expression tends to be vague and rhetorical, and often seems to be applied in contradictory ways. That is because the justice that is served by the law is a reflection of moral and cultural values. As our society becomes more and more culturally diverse, values are not always shared. What may appear as justice to one person is not justice to another. There is rarely, if ever, a common perception of justice any more than there is a common perception of facts. Aspects of the justice system are invariably perceived by someone to be unjust. Justice is not absolute, although we often desire it to be so.

Justice, as a legal concept, is a popular vehicle to put into service to reinforce our judgment. We seek to resolve conflict by judging that someone is to blame for what has happened. While we also credit justice when we recognize that the wrong person has been blamed, usually the blame is then shifted onto someone else. A call for justice can be a plea that others judge me or someone else as innocent. Or it can be a call

---

[23] This is an excerpt from the judgment of Lamer J. in *Reference re Section 94(2) of the Motor Vehicle Act (B.C.)*, [1985] 2 S.C.R. 486 at 503.

[24] Ibid.

to judge someone as guilty. Either way, justice is predicated on the belief that there are victims and victimizers in the world, and that our peace depends on judging who is acting out which role.

Because law is so heavily steeped in the language of fairness, and because it places so much emphasis on procedural protection in order to avoid judging wrongly, it is a vehicle that is particularly well-suited to express our passion for vengeance. This is essentially what our thoughts of justice boil down to. It is easy to feel justified in projecting our own guilt and anger onto others when the framework in which we do it has such an aura of respectability, authority and dedication to fairness.

To understand the concept of "justice" in spiritual terms has required that I let go of everything I ever thought or learned about justice in the world. Justice is not about "doing" something to someone else; it is not about passing judgment on someone else. It is about releasing my own judgment and opening my mind to seeing the *injustice* of the attack that my judgment represents. Justice is a Divine correction of my attraction to injustice, and is accessible only through my willingness to forgive.[25] Justice is the gift of healing.

---

[25] It is expressed this way in *A Course in Miracles*:

"God's Judgment is His justice. Onto this, - a Judgment wholly lacking in condemnation; an evaluation based entirely on love, - you have projected your injustice, giving God the lens of warped perception through which you look." - Manual for Teachers, p. 47-8.
"Vengeance is alien to God's mind *because* He knows of justice. To be just is to be fair, and not be vengeful. Fairness and vengeance are impossible, for each one contradicts the other and denies that it is real." -Text, p. 498.

It follows that when I use the law and the legal system as a means of judging, attacking and controlling others, I am susceptible to experiencing conflict, resentment and anger and, depending upon the outcome, dissatisfaction with the system. The law cannot nourish my desire to judge and control, and at the same time serve the cause of healing.

To look for justice in the institutional judgments of the legal system, and in the outcomes of the myriad cases that have been decided within that system, is, at least from my own spiritual vantage point, to be looking in the wrong place. The justice of which I speak, which flows from forgiveness, is difficult to find in the outward trappings of the legal system. Even our notion of "pardon" assumes the "guilt" of the one who is pardoned of a crime, and is granted only after prescribed conditions have been satisfied.

The hope for true justice, I believe, resides in the individual choices that are made each and every day by those who administer the system. Those who choose to do their jobs in the spirit of love and true empathy, rather than in judgment, experience the taste of justice in the Divine sense of which I have spoken.

Our sense of justice in the world is directed not only at those whom we accuse, "rightly" or "wrongly," of transgressing the laws of the world; things sometimes happen that cause us to perceive the system itself as unjust. Our focus may be diverted from meting out "justice" (in the form of judgment) to offenders, to judging and attacking the system itself and those who run it. And how, you may ask, could we *not* condemn a system that would wrongly imprison men like Donald Marshall and the Birmingham Six for substantial segments of their lives, or that discriminates against minority groups such as Indians and blacks? How could we not call out for justice to be done?

I am not suggesting that we should not ask for justice in those situations. What I am suggesting is that we should examine where and how we look for justice, and how we think about it. Do we find it in our moral indignation and judgment about what seems to have been done to us or to others with whom we identify? Does that bring justice to anyone? Does it bring healing, peace or love? Those who feel wronged cannot reverse what has happened; and they may not be able to prevent it from happening again, either to themselves or someone else. They can, however, heal the conflict they are experiencing and find peace, if they choose forgiveness. And so can the rest of us who react so vehemently to these seeming injustices.

For Donald Marshall, the "Birmingham Six" and the many others who have mistakenly been adjudged "guilty" in the legal systems of the world, the ordeals through which they have gone in securing their release from incarceration have unquestionably raised tremendous conflict, not only for themselves but for their families, friends and lawyers, for empathizing observers, as well as for all those who are accused of perpetrating the injustices, along with their own support networks. Far be it from me to minimize the effort and discipline that is required of anyone to see beyond the powerful emotions that arise in such circumstances. At the same time, their experiences offer dramatic opportunities for healing through forgiveness, and for feeling the gentleness of true justice. For all of us who are touched in different ways by these events there is a path to healing that may as yet be unexplored. We can see justice as something more than the verdict of innocence that our legal system has now bestowed upon them. We can see justice in a different light as we come into touch with their true innocence.

Some of our greatest frustrations with law and the legal system surround the concept of justice, and the seeming lack of it in so many quarters. Stories of injustice abound, and our fears that we ourselves will be treated unjustly warp our impressions of the legal system. There is a strong desire to fix the system, to remould it and to better control it to strengthen our sense of justice. Undoubtedly, we can change the law here and "improve" it there; but to place our hopes for justice in simply changing the law and the legal system to meet our varied perceptions of what is fair and just in particular circumstances, or to promote the answer as lying in the adoption of alternative dispute resolution processes in lieu of the traditional courts, is to miss important lessons that the system, even in its present imperfect state, offers to teach us: that peace and healing lie in forgiveness, not in judgment; and that justice is experienced in peace, not in attack. By applying those lessons as we use the law, and as we reform the law to meet new and changing social conditions, we are contributing to the experience of a more just legal system than the one we currently have.

As we give up judgment we begin to see justice.

## PUNISHMENT

The law sees punishment as serving three main roles: retribution, which demands that offenders pay for the harm they have caused; deterrence, which is to control others by warning them of what could happen to them if they should transgress the law; and value reinforcement, which is to remind all of us of the ideas that are prized most highly in our society. The first is imposed out of vengeance, the second out of fear, and the third in the belief that values can be taught through negative reinforcement.

From a spiritual perspective, it is impossible to reconcile forgiveness with punishment, whatever its purpose may be:

"The sight of innocence makes punishment impossible... ."[26]

A dominant symbol of punishment in the Christian culture is that of Jesus dying on the cross. Seen as punishment, it is the ultimate symbol of our imprisonment by illusions. Many people have come to look at that event instead as a symbol of release, of rebirth, and of the ability of each of us to understand and experience our spiritual unity in the face of seemingly unbearable pain and suffering. Those who truly believe in their innocence cannot be punished.

To perceive a situation as punishment reflects a state of mind. Any of life's situations, a job, an illness, even a marriage, can be perceived as punishment. A criminal sentence, which is normally seen as punishment, can also be seen as an

---

[26] *A Course in Miracles*, Text, p. 502.

opportunity for healing, for learning, for getting in touch with one's essence and with one's function in the world. It is *we* who give the law over to the perceptions of punishment. And it is we who can liberate the law from the constraints of those perceptions by seeing differently, whether looking from the vantage point of the one who imposes the criminal sentence, or from that of the person who is subjected to it.

Many criminal offenders have succeeded in turning their lives around by learning to find the blessings in their situations, and by experiencing renewed hope. The criminal justice system presents choices for people, not only those who are the objects of punishment, but also those who are called upon to administer the system. They may be difficult choices, but they are no less choices than those encountered in other experiences.

Whenever we speak of punishment it is helpful, particularly from the standpoint of those who are the objects of the law's judgment, to remember the lesson of Jesus. No matter how vindictive our society may seem to be, those who are required and expected to "suffer" the punishment have the capacity to see differently the experience they are undergoing. Through forgiveness, punishment evaporates and is replaced by an opportunity for healing. Nowhere have I seen it more powerfully stated than in this passage expressed through the mind and pen of Victor Hugo:

The Bishop looked at him and said:

"You have suffered much?"

"Oh! the red jacket, the cannon-ball on the ankle, a plank to sleep on, heat, cold, toil, blows, the double chain for a nothing, a dungeon for a word; even sick and in bed, the chain-gang. The very dogs are happier. Nineteen years! Now I am forty-six; and at present the yellow passport! There it is!"

"Yes," said the Bishop, "you have come from a very sad place. Listen. There will be more joy in heaven over the tearful face of a repentant sinner than over the white robes of a hundred just men. If you leave that mournful place with thoughts of hatred and anger against your fellow men you are worthy of pity; if you leave it with thoughts of good will and of peace you are more worthy than any of us."

Victor Hugo, *Les Miserables*

For most of us, that lesson is learned only with considerable difficulty. We search uncertainly for the innocence we share with others, and we continue to experience as punishment the sentences that are imposed by our judges. There remains a strong investment in punishment, both from the standpoint of society, and from the standpoint of the ones who are sentenced.

Nonetheless, arising out of the growing recognition of human dignity and human rights in our society and in our law, we have seen the rejection in modern times of certain forms of punishment that were once considered acceptable, for example torture, corporal punishment (e.g. whipping) and lifetime incarceration. We have also seen the emergence of the concept of corrections. The word "corrections" is often applied to the branch of criminal justice that comprises rehabilitation and parole. Opportunities are extended to prisoners to demonstrate their willingness to look differently at themselves and their situations in the world, and to start over again at a point before their sentences have fully elapsed. These concepts override sentencing, so that even "lifers" are, in the ordinary course, eligible at some point for release before their sentences have run their full course. Significant public resources are committed to this end, and many prisoners over the years have benefitted from correctional programs.

The law's idea of correction remains, nonetheless, rooted in a strong belief in the value of punishment. To the extent it reflects a form of forgiveness, as the world sees it, it must be "earned" by exhibiting a spirit of reform. And so, although in one sense it affirms the inherent worth and potential of everyone, in another sense it denies that worth by offering it only conditional recognition.

True correction occurs in an atmosphere of forgiveness, not anger, fear and judgment. It comes from within; it is not imposed from outside.[27] Although it is open to us to accept the role of teacher and to serve as channels through which another may come to receive and accept correction, it is not for us to impose correction on another. I have no doubt that this is understood by many of those who work within the correctional system and who bring to their responsibilities the true empathy or compassion that comes from looking beyond the institutional trappings and prejudices of the system to the inherent worth of the individuals they serve. By supporting their clients, they

---

[27] This idea is expressed in the following quotation from *A Course in Miracles*, Text, p. 156: "Any attempt you make to correct a brother means that you believe correction by you is possible, and this can only be the arrogance of the ego. Correction is of God, Who does not know of arrogance."

nurture growth from within. We can learn from these teachers to see differently.

Among the most difficult issues relating to punishment are those that surround the death penalty. Canada abolished the death penalty for all but a few military offences in 1976. In 1987, in the face of renewed calls for the reinstatement of capital punishment for certain forms of murder, in particular for killing police officers, Parliament, by a narrow margin on a free vote, reaffirmed its earlier decision to abolish the death penalty. Canada has also subscribed to numerous international agreements that support the abolition of capital punishment. The Canadian position is in accord with the public policy of a growing list of countries in the western world, and, more recently, in eastern Europe.

Some of the states of the United States, on the other hand, continue to impose the death penalty in some cases. There has been no national consensus emerging in that country to abolish the death penalty.

The difference between the law and policy of Canada and the United States on this issue was highlighted in two recent cases involving questions concerning extradition (i.e. the return of fugitives).[28] Two fugitives from the United States, one a convicted murderer, Joseph Kindler, and the other, Charles Ng, who was wanted on charges of multiple murder, were arrested in Canada. The United States sought extradition, as is provided for in a treaty to which both countries are parties, and in a

---

[28] The decisions in *Kindler v. Canada (Minister of Justice)* and *Reference Re Ng Extradition* were handed down by the Supreme Court of Canada on September 26, 1991.

Canadian statute.

Without going into too much detail about the cases, let me just say that the narrow issue was whether or not the Minister of Justice for Canada should have exercised his statutory discretion to extradite these men to the United States to be dealt with in accordance with the United States justice system, without seeking assurances that they would not face the death penalty. Kindler had already been sentenced to death, and Ng faces the death penalty if convicted of the charges against him. The argument centered around the idea that if these men could not, because of the *Canadian Charter of Rights and Freedoms*, be sentenced to death in Canada for similar crimes if committed in Canada, it offended their rights to be sent back to the United States to face death. Not only was it argued that this amounted to a double standard on this fundamental moral issue, the position advanced was that it violated Canadian law as well as Canada's international commitments for the government to send them back without having asked for and received assurances that the death penalty would not be imposed.

Four of the judges, constituting the majority, took a somewhat pragmatic approach. The United States, not Canada, was imposing the punishment; Canada would be exposing itself as a haven for fugitives if it refused to send them back without assurances; to refuse to send them back could prejudice Canada's efforts to secure extradition of its own fugitives in the future; and, in any event, the death penalty was not seen to be so morally outrageous to Canadians as to warrant a refusal to extradite, particularly in light of the strong liberal and democratic traditions of the United States' justice system. We live in a complex and imperfect world and, as Canadians, we cannot always impose our collective moral values on others. For the majority, the issue was less about the morality and constitutionality of the death penalty under Canadian law than it was about the practical realities of enforcing criminal law in the international community.

The dissenting judges addressed the issues more as a matter of principle, and held that capital punishment was "cruel and unusual punishment" and thus prohibited by the *Canadian Charter of Rights and Freedoms.* [Interestingly, cruel and unusual punishments are also forbidden by the Eighth amendment to the United States Constitution.[29]] For the Minister to exercise his discretion to extradite without seeking assurances was to subject Kindler and Ng to cruel and unusual punishment.

My purpose is not to engage in detailed analysis of, or to argue in favour of or against, the positions and approaches exhibited in the majority and minority positions of the Supreme Court of Canada; there is much to be said in support of each. Rather, what the cases offer for me is a context in which I can explore, at least to a limited extent, how the issues surrounding the death penalty relate to the broader issues of punishment.

On the one hand, the fact that the issues often arise in cases involving heinous crimes committed by people we are inclined to disassociate from humanity, attracts support for the "justice" of the death penalty. It is not easy for most of us to see the innocence of people like Kindler and Ng, and to forgive

---

[29] It is also interesting to note that the United States Supreme Court has not held the death penalty to be unconstitutional as cruel and unusual punishment: *Glass v. Louisiana,* 471 U.S. 1080 (1985).

them for their "crimes."

On the other hand, the death penalty is a particularly difficult form of punishment for many people to accept because of the strong attachment to life and the widespread fear of death that seem to grip our society. The *Canadian Charter of Rights and Freedoms*[30] entrenches a right to life, and it is not surprising that to impose death as a "punishment" should be seen *prima facie* as an affront to that right.

However, not everyone looks at death in the same way. Those who see in the death of the body the end of our existence may view the death penalty more harshly than those who see in death, as in all experiences, an element of choice, at some level, to move into a different dimension of our existence.

Some people may focus on the *manner* in which death is imposed. To inflict death with suffering or torture may seem cruel and unusual, whereas to inflict it with compassion and sensitivity, as for example in euthanasia, would not be. I think it is important to recognize that to inflict death on another is not always an attack. It is our attitude, our judgment, that gives it that character.

For some, the forced imposition of death will be "the ultimate indignity." For others it will not be. It is unlikely that a broad consensus about the subject of death could be found in today's society, apart from the fact that most people seem to entertain a lot of fear about it. Fears about their own deaths,

---

[30] In particular, section 7, referred to above in the discussion of Justice, protects "life, liberty and security of the person." This is somewhat akin to "life, liberty and the pursuit of happiness," which is protected in the Constitution of the United States.

and those of loved ones, by the hands of "criminals," may strengthen the willingness of many to impose the death penalty, either as deterrence or as retribution. At the same time, I suspect that fears about death support the attraction others have to *abolishing* the death penalty.

We have come as far as we have in reforming our attitudes towards both capital and corporal punishment because of the commitment certain individuals over the years have held towards the essential values that underscore our humanness. Strong expressions of principle, such as those found in the dissenting judgment of Mr. Justice Cory in the cases dealing with Kindler and Ng, are, for that reason, admirable. However, in our eagerness to eliminate death and other severe forms of punishment, we can lose sight of the issues at a more fundamental level. In particular, it is important not to lose sight of the spiritual notion with which I began this discussion: "The sight of innocence makes punishment impossible." To seek refuge in any form of punishment is to surrender to our fears; it is the manifestation of our unwillingness to look for and to find the love within us and in others.

Each time we confront the prospect of punishment, our own or someone else's, we are offered the opportunity for healing, to look at our beliefs, and at our own illusions, in a forgiving light. In this context, I see no difference between the death penalty and any other form of punishment. There is no heirarchy of illusions. It may seem morally appropriate to oppose the *death penalty*, in view of the supreme value our society places on life. But does that really address the issue of punishment at its more fundamental level? In the end, punishment in any form, capital or otherwise, is about judgment.

To substitute one punishment for another does nothing to recognize the spiritual innocence of the one on whom the punishment is imposed. Whatever be its form, if I am seeing it as "punishment," I am using it to support my judgment.

The judgment that imprisons us, and that we seem to experience all around us, is our own. As long as I, as an individual, am prepared to look upon what is done to another or to myself as punishment, my judgment will impede my search for the innocence that will heal me. The first step towards a more compassionate world, therefore, is the one *I* take. In that sense, "seeing law differently" begins with a change within myself, which leads to seeing differently, through the eyes of forgiveness not judgment, the world in which law operates. The law requires each of us to do certain things in the world, and it seeks to influence our attitudes. But the law does not, and cannot, dictate how we see it and how we use it. It is not the language or letter of the law that keeps us in judgment. It is our own beliefs about ourselves that we have projected onto the world.

Reflection about capital punishment is useful, therefore, insofar as it leads us to reexamine our attitudes towards punishment in its broadest forms. As we learn to give up our beliefs about the merits of punishment, we open to the possibility of true correction, and the healing that comes from the awareness of our essential innocence.

I think that, in moving towards a clearer awareness of our essential innocence, we shall continue to struggle, as a society and as individuals, with the scope and meaning of "cruel and unusual punishment" and its relation to death and other forms of punishment. What may seem perfectly acceptable to us today may at another time give rise to issues that are reminiscent of those that are being debated today concerning the death penalty. As we learn to be more forgiving, however, we become attuned to a different sense of reality. Ultimately, forgiveness negates punishment in all its forms.

## PART III - FUNCTIONS

I am here only to be truly helpful.
I am here to represent Him Who sent me.
I do not have to worry about what to say
or what to do, because He Who sent me
will direct me.
I am content to be wherever He wishes,
knowing He goes there with me.
I will be healed as I let Him teach me to heal.

*A Course in Miracles*, Text, page 24.

## LAWYERS AND CLIENTS

One of the gateways to healing is the lawyer and client relationship. And yet, forgiveness is not an easy subject to approach in this relationship. By the time many people reach the point they are willing to talk to a lawyer about their legal problems, they are already in the grip of fear and desperation. They feel the authority of the law breathing down their necks, and they feel vulnerable. They perceive their interests to be threatened. It is much easier for lawyers to respond in ways that are aggressively sympathetic with their clients, even though that usually has the effect of reinforcing the client's fear of, and sense of separation from, the person who is perceived to be at the root of the problem.

Lawyers and clients react to meet their mutual expectations of each other. And thus the attack syndrome is fuelled. We have great difficulty accepting, as individuals and as a society, that control does not work, that it does not solve problems, that it does not make people happy. We fear that our society will be overrun by criminals if we relinquish control; we fear that our neighbours will take advantage of us. Pragmatically speaking, forgiveness is a difficult concept to import into the legal system.

What I am speaking about, however, is not reform of institutional policy or process, so much as reform of our own attitudes to the process in which we find ourselves as lawyers and clients. It is open to each of us to make a personal choice to see law differently, to see the legal system and legal process differently, and to see those with whom we come into contact differently, whether they are working inside the legal system looking out, or outside the system looking in. It is open to each of us to see problems in a different light, and to help others to see them in a way that is conducive to healing. I am convinced that many people do that intuitively, without reference to any analytical framework such as I am presenting in this book. For those who, like me, do not respond as easily at an intuitive level, a structured approach may help in gaining an understanding of what is involved in approaching legal situations, and lawyer/client relationships, in this different light.

What practical steps can I, as a lawyer, take that may respond in a positive way to the call for help that my client's visit to my office represents? What can I do to avoid reinforcing the fear that underlies the problem my client is relating to me? Here are some thoughts I try to keep in mind. They may not be relevant in every situation, but overall they help me in dealing even with situations that I might never have dreamed bore any relation to healing. Later I shall make some complementary suggestions that clients might consider, to help bring lawyers into touch with the process that the lawyer/client relationship presents to them.

1. It is helpful for me to respect the integrity of my client's healing process. I am there to help facilitate that process, to provide information and advice on legal questions, and to execute certain matters, but not to assume the overall management of the conflict and its solution.

People in today's society are presented continuously, in almost every situation, with the opportunity to hand over their problems to someone else, whether it be to doctors, lawyers, teachers, the police, contractors, plumbers or mechanics. The service industry invites, and prospers from, this delegation of responsibility. With some matters it may be possible to do this, but not when it comes to healing. Until we accept the responsibility for what underlies the seeming legal difficulty we have with someone else, we are unlikely to find a path to its solution. Handing the problem over to a lawyer in the form of a "legal" problem is not the answer. It only brings on more frustration and resentment. Lawyers can be sensitive to this, and can explain to clients how and where they fit into the process, what they can do and what they cannot do.

2.      I can try to listen more closely to what my client is telling me. There are effective listening techniques that apply not just in lawyer/client relationships, but in all relationships. Some of the biggest barriers to effective listening are:

-       ordering, directing or commanding clients to do certain things;
-       warning or threatening clients that if they do not do something, something terrible is going to happen;
-       moralizing, preaching, or imploring clients to do something *I* feel they should do;
-       advising, or offering suggestions or solutions before clients are ready for them;
-       attempting to persuade clients of *my* point of view with logic, lecture and argument;
-       judging, criticizing, disagreeing with or blaming clients for things they tell me they have done, or have not done;
-       conversely, praising, agreeing with or buttering up clients;

- along the same lines, reassuring, sympathizing with, consoling or supporting clients in ways that simply reinforce their negative views of themselves. Depending on the context, it may appear condescending. Alternatively, it may reinforce ideas a client is trying to release;
- continuously interrupting clients with probing, questioning, interrogating. This may distract clients from telling me what they are really seeing;
- making light of what clients may consider to be serious points;
- distracting or diverting clients when explaining the situation to me, or engaging in light-hearted kidding about their problems.[31]

Many of the things lawyers take for granted can be barriers to true communication when engaging in conversation with clients. When lawyers interrupt to structure the interview, it is usually the lawyer's agenda, not the client's agenda, that is being served. The very fact of having to communicate with a lawyer can be intimidating for clients. Lawyers can try to make clients feel at ease and relaxed, and that what they are saying is important, relevant, useful and worth listening to. For the lawyer to attempt to focus the interview too early is to take charge of the process, releasing the client from the responsibility for it, rather than reinforcing that responsibility.

---

[31] This is my adaptation of a list of twelve barriers to effective listening compiled by Dr. Thomas Gordon in his *Leader Effectiveness Training*.

3.  I can ascertain what my clients want to use the law and the legal system to accomplish. Do they have specific outcomes in mind (e.g. to obtain custody of the children), or do they only want to know what their legal positions are, generally? Do they believe that their desired legal outcomes are fair and just?

4.  I can try to explain, without giving advice too early as to how the problem should be resolved, what the law has to say about the circumstances and about the questions my clients have put to me. For example, if the matter should go to court, how is a judge likely to look at the situation, recognizing that there are many factors that will affect a judge's attitude?

5.  I can try to ascertain whether or not my clients' expectations about outcomes have been modified at all by my feedback. How flexible do my clients appear to be about their expectations? Do they express or indicate any resentment or concern about my feedback on the law?

6.  I can ascertain whether my clients have made their expectations about outcomes known to the other parties. Have the other parties made their expectations known? Do I perceive judgment in my clients directed towards other parties and/or their positions? Do my clients exhibit any willingness to let go of their judgment, if they could be helped to do that? Without suggesting to clients that this is what they *should* do, I can try to find out whether or not there is at least a little willingness to give up judgment.

7.  I can ascertain whether or not my clients are willing to

deal with other parties personally. If there is a history of animosity between the parties, this may be difficult. It may be necessary to locate resources/contacts to help me to prepare clients to do this in a way that is likely to ameliorate, rather than exacerbate, communication between the parties.

8.      I can ascertain whether or not my clients are willing to talk about their situations from a spiritual perspective. If so, it may facilitate the identification, acceptance and ultimate release of blocks that are in the way of an effective solution. These are the familiar ego blocks of fear and guilt that attract us towards the attachments that imprison us in so many areas of our lives. Again, this is an area in which other resources and contacts can help, if clients are prepared to look at their problems in this light.

If a client is unwilling or unable to look beneath the "problem" to its spiritual underpinnings, or is not interested in even advancing a position that is seen as fair and just, I may find myself with a client who is clearly and unabashedly seeking to use the law as a means of attacking or controlling someone else. I may have a strong temptation to judge my client. This highlights the importance of my acknowledging my own healing process. Just as I, as a lawyer, can serve as a facilitator in my client's healing process, every client, and every situation presented by a client, affords me an opportunity for healing. The manner in which I respond to that opportunity will have a significant bearing on my effectiveness as a lawyer in facilitating the healing process of my client. Thus, the relationship is a reciprocal one.

I have observed over the years that many lawyers, perhaps most, do not accept that their clients' problems have anything to do with themselves. They regard themselves as service providers. They refuse to identify with, or to become involved in, their clients' problems. " Tell the clients what to do, as best you can, but don't get involved! Keep your distance! Maintain a professional relationship!" And yet, the lawyers who seem to be happiest in their work, and most dedicated, are those who *do* become involved with their clients and relate to them and their problems as people, not as technicians. This involvement is part of the lawyer's own healing process.

In my experience, lawyer/client relations has been a neglected area of legal training. The assumption seems to have been that if lawyers are educated as sound legal technicians, and if they are drilled in the bare essentials of legal ethics, they can function effectively as legal advisers and advocates. There is little or no recognition that lawyers, who deal daily with relationship problems, can be as instrumental in healing as doctors, nurses, dentists, psychologists, teachers and others in the helping professions. Lawyers carry out their trade with little or no training in communication skills or psychological methods. Many lawyers are attentive to the lawyer/client relationship mainly with a view to its business potential, rather than to developing an effective working relationship that will be of true service to clients. As lawyers, we might ask ourselves questions such as these:

- Are we really listening to our clients?
- Do we find ourselves judging our clients?
- Do we find ourselves judging other parties, other

lawyers, judges, administrators?

- Are we preoccupied with "winning" cases and with upgrading our image as someone who gets "results" for our clients?
- Do we tend to rate our files as "good" and "bad" ones, depending on how much conflict working on the files brings up for us? Do we project our negative attitudes onto certain files, either procrastinating from dealing with matters that should be dealt with, or sloughing off the problems onto junior lawyers?
- Are we preoccupied with fees, and with justifying our fees to our clients?
- Do we sometimes put the interests of our clients behind our own?
- Do we see our clients as brothers and sisters, as equal participants and as teachers and learners in the situation that our lawyer/client relationship presents to us, or do we presume to provide preemptive solutions to our clients' problems?
- Do we feel threatened or critical when our clients do not follow our advice?

To many lawyers, the concepts of forgiveness and healing may seem somewhat foreign. And that's all right. To others, however, the idea may not seem as radical and far reaching. There are those who may see, in the dimension of "law reform" that I am presenting in this book, relief from the frustrations of working in a profession that often seems to cripple our faculties for experiencing joy, peace, harmony and happiness in our lives.

There is, of course, fear: fear of being different, of being criticized, of being honest, of reaching out to touch someone, of being seen as weak and unrealistic, of not having clients who are receptive to these approaches, of not being understood. I experience those fears. It is easy to tell myself that this is not what being a lawyer is all about. And yet, to be invited to see differently, to see my relationships with my clients as opportunities to work through our respective processes of conflict resolution, opens up a new dimension of service grounded in a commitment to healing.

Doubts will be expressed as to whether one could adopt such an approach and survive in the "big business" atmosphere in which law is practiced today, particularly in large firms. Typically, lawyers are expected to docket anywhere from 1,500 to 2,000 billable hours a year at high billing rates. This is necessary to cover each lawyer's share of the significant overhead involved in running a modern law firm, and to generate enough profit to support the levels of income that lawyers have come to expect for their work. That alone, apart from the intensity of the work lawyers do, creates high stress within the profession. A law firm can provide a relatively fear-filled environment in which to function.

Additional pressure is imposed by the fact that the practicing lawyer usually has partners and associates, and they may not share the same philosophy and goals. There may be doubts expressed about the nature of the practice the "reformed" lawyer is carrying on, and his or her commitment to the goals and the culture of the firm, not to mention the contribution to the "bottom line." Some colleagues more than others will appreciate the nature and extent of the lawyer's contribution.

In principle, none of that should deter the lawyer from his or her spiritual path, which is there to lead its traveller in peace through chaos and adversity. This does not imply, however, that the forms within which the lawyer is to function will remain constant. It may be possible to practice law in a conventional environment, and it may not.

As well, it may be easier to integrate the approach I have described into some areas of practice than into others. A great deal depends, I think, on the confidence the lawyer has in his or her ability to practice in this way, and in his or her willingness to assume the role of teacher to others. It always seems easier to function in an environment of like-minded people, and many will prefer this to working within a more conventional legal culture. All of this involves choices along the way, which may have, among other things, economic implications for the lawyer who is true to his or her spiritual path.

I want to stress, however, that there is nowhere one can be, and nothing one can do, that precludes functioning in a loving, non-judgmental frame of mind. Such an attitude cannot fail to make an enormous contribution to any environment in which one works. Everything I have talked about in this discussion in terms of techniques and approaches flows from that attitude. To make the commitment to that attitude when relating to everyone, whether fellow lawyers, clients, judges, witnesses, secretaries or administrators, in every situation you encounter in day to day practice, is the most important step. It leads into a different world, a world in which the more you give the more you receive.

Clients who have a willingness to see law differently can help to manifest a new vision of "lawyering" by helping lawyers to accept responsibility for their own processes, just as I am inviting lawyers to help clients accept responsibility for theirs. It behooves clients to become more open about their expectations of their lawyers, and to ask themselves the same kinds of questions as I am inviting lawyers to ask. How much judgment are clients hanging on to? How honest are they about their expectations? Do clients prefer to retain lawyers who will nurture their material desires of "winning big," who will fight to put their opponents in their places, and who will use the law to attack and control? Or are clients willing to work with a lawyer who is committed to healing? Are clients willing to give up their attachment to "getting?" Are they prepared to tell their lawyers about their commitment?

In my view, it is only after coming to grips with those fundamental, and admittedly difficult, questions that lawyers and clients can effectively work together to explore the various options for truly resolving the conflict the client is experiencing. The "form" of the process, i.e. whether it be litigation, arbitration or some other form of adjudication, or mediation, negotiation or other kinds or combinations of processes, is less important than the "content": i.e. where is the client coming from? Where is the lawyer coming from? Are they working together towards shared goals? Are they truly experiencing a forgiving attitude to each other, to the circumstances, to the process, to the system, to the other parties and players? If they are not yet experiencing this, are they at least committed to the *goal* of forgiveness?

If the lawyer and client are not in the same space, and are not sharing the same goal, or if one is leading the other in a direction that the other does not feel comfortable in following, the conflict the client is experiencing will be more difficult to resolve. The "legal problem" may eventually be taken care of, but the client's experience is unlikely to be one of healing.

I am not suggesting that it is *essential* for a client who seeks to heal the conflict underlying a legal dispute with another person to seek out a lawyer who can facilitate this process. But it can certainly help. Lawyers who are willing to acknowledge that the legal process can serve higher goals than winning are encouraged to explore these goals with their clients, through the approaches and techniques I have suggested above. If healing is of concern to either of the parties to the relationship, i.e. either the lawyer or the client, and that party fails openly to acknowledge that concern, then the relationship may fail to realize the full opportunity it holds out to them. For this reason, it is important for both lawyers and clients to be open and honest about their expectations.

I recently had lunch with a businessman, Tom, who related to me how his efforts at building a company culture around love-based business and management principles seemed to be frustrated every time his lawyer became involved in a transaction, whether it be the hiring of an employee or negotiations with another company. Tom complained about the aggressive posture assumed by this lawyer in virtually every situation, and how difficult the lawyer would become whenever Tom would choose not to follow his advice. It seemed to Tom as though the lawyer was either oblivious to his aspirations for a particular business style, or was unable to let go of the control that lawyers are accustomed to assuming in these relationships. Of course, I have no way of evaluating the situation from the lawyer's point of view, and my purpose in relating the anecdote is not to pass judgment on what may have contributed to Tom's perception of the relationship. It struck me, however, that these relationships, like any other relationship, stop working when there is not a shared goal, when the lawyer, for whatever reason, is unable to tune into the rhythm of the client, and vice versa.

Tom contrasted that experience with the first matter he had handed over to his new law firm, a complaint alleging that his company had infringed a patent. When the letter of response arrived from the lawyer for Tom's signature, it was written in a traditional, lawyerly, attack-defence style. Tom decided to rewrite the letter in a more positive tone, seeing a potential business opportunity hidden in the complaint. Having sent the redrafted letter back to the lawyer for review, he cringed when the inevitable telephone call came, expecting to be attacked for the changes he had deigned to make. Happily, the response was agreeable and the letter went out as redrafted.

The story illustrated to me, first, how important it is for lawyers and clients to work together and for the client not to relinquish responsibility for the process. Rather than resigning himself to accepting advice with which he was not really satisfied, and projecting his upset onto his lawyer, Tom was willing to do something that made him feel better about the situation. He is still struggling with the dynamics of the new relationship, but seems to me to be open to the idea of learning from his experiences and of working to educate his new lawyer to appreciate his style and his needs. His first dealings turned out in the end to be positive, and he is optimistic that a good relationship will result.

The story also illustrates how easy it is to turn situations from problems into opportunities. Had it not been for Tom's initiative, the letter might have gone out as originally formulated, which would not, at least in Tom's mind, have served the interests of the company any more than it would have advanced the prospects of an effective relationship with his new lawyers. The language and culture of the law tends to focus on problems, not opportunities. The simple rephrasing of a sentence in a letter can make a world of difference in the relationship between parties who perceive themselves as being at odds with each other. Rather than offering someone an ultimatum or an outright rejection, you can offer them an opportunity. As lawyers, we often become so caught up in our self-images and in our narrow perceptions of client expectations that we miss opportunities to serve our clients in productive ways. There is a useful lesson here for all of us.

In that regard, I do not believe that a lawyer's commitment to healing is dependent on having clients, such as Tom, who are openly searching for someone who practices law from a healing perspective. The commitment can be expressed in every situation in which a lawyer is called upon to serve. I see my role as a lawyer as coming down to these essential elements: First, it is to help clients to understand what the law enables and requires them to do in particular situations. Where do they stand in the eyes of the law? In some cases this will be reasonably clear. In other cases it will be uncertain, either because of ambiguities in the law or because of confusion or disagreement about the facts. In every situation there will be choices to make, some of which will appear to have more detrimental impact than others upon my client. As a lawyer, I can facilitate the process of making those choices. That is, I think, a fair description of how lawyers have generally viewed their role, and how most people would look upon it. Facilitating choices is certainly an important aspect of "lawyering," and one I would not presume to change.

Second, I see it as my role to help clients make these choices in ways that bring healing in every situation. It may involve nothing more than explaining to someone what the law requires of them in particular circumstances and helping them to comply without feeling victimized by the government or by the person to whom they have undertaken an obligation. It may be as simple as helping them to feel accepting of and comfortable with their legal obligations, looking at them as positive and not negative reinforcements in their lives.

In that regard, I must admit that I sometimes have a tendency to feel "put upon," especially by the government, as laws become more pervasive and ever more complex and costly to comply with. I can feel my own pain begin to well up as I look at the complexity of a municipal or administrative process or as I feel the bite of a new or increased tax a government has imposed. I find myself becoming quite judgmental until I consciously step back and observe how unproductive and self-defeating that really is. And so, being a lawyer often amounts to openly sharing with a client feelings about laws that affect both of us. We are involved jointly in a process of changing our attitudes about those laws, learning to understand them better, learning to work in a positive way with the people who administer them, and learning to accept and to honour our obligations under them. It is important in this process to remember that as lawyers and clients we teach and learn from each other.

My role as a lawyer also requires me to help clients to

make choices about their "rights." My commitment is to help them make those choices in a way that brings the greatest amount of healing to everyone affected. I see this as an even greater challenge than helping clients to understand and accept their obligations. In focusing on their rights, clients are seeing their pain and loss being caused by someone else's failure to meet their legal obligations. It is easy to look upon oneself as a victim in such circumstances and to use one's rights to respond to those feelings. I see my role as a lawyer as being to help clients to see their situations in a more forgiving light, rather than reinforcing their feelings of anger and resentment towards the person who has seemingly violated their rights.

Third, I see it as my role to maintain a positive attitude towards my clients and everyone I have to deal with on their behalf. I do not see it as my role to attack people on behalf of my clients, any more than I see it as helpful for my clients to be attacking others on their own behalf. Because it may be difficult at times for clients to understand how I can be forgiving towards those who are causing them so much grief, it is essential for me to take the time to explain to them why it is I see that as being so important.

Boiled down to those three elements, the role I have described may not seem as radically different from the conventional conception of a lawyer's role as it may have seemed at first blush. My role is certainly not to persuade clients to join me on my spiritual path. It is simply to allow myself to be guided by my spiritual direction to help clients to see their situations in a different light. I realize that many people can be quite uncomfortable with "spiritual stuff," and may have difficulty looking at their situations as a growth process. In that regard, I have found that I can focus on "attitude" without being overtly spiritual, as long as I am not misleading my clients about where I am coming from. In the final analysis, many of the techniques and approaches I have described in this discussion are those that can be used effectively to enhance relationships even with established and seemingly traditional clients and in conventional areas of legal practice. To a large extent they can be used even by lawyers who may be reluctant to embrace the full dimensions of the spiritual basis of the approach I am describing.

In the end, effective "lawyering" requires more than competence. Attitude is crucial. In that vein, I, and no one else, am responsible for my attitude. My attitude as a lawyer is bound to influence how my client looks at whatever situation we are addressing together. If I am committed to helping my clients change their attitudes, I must first be committed to changing my own. That, in a nutshell, is the focus and the force of my commitment to healing.

# THE JUDICIARY

Recently I watched the award winning film "Separate but Equal," which was a dramatization of events leading up to the landmark decision of the United States Supreme Court in 1953 in the school desegregation cases.[32] The film began with the story of one of the plaintiffs, a black child by the name of Harry Briggs, who was forced to walk five miles to school and back each day because there was no school bus for black children to service his school. The schools which black children attended were significantly lacking in facilities, as compared with the schools provided for white children. The tax dollars allocated per child for black schools was less than one quarter of that allocated for white schools. There was little doubt that the situation was in violation of the state constitution of South Carolina. Although that constitution prescribed that education must be offered on a segregated basis, it also demanded equality of facilities as between white and black schools.

Through the dedication and commitment of a number of persons in the local black community, and the preparedness of ordinary black citizens to assert their constitutional rights in the face of strong resistance from the white community (some blacks lost their jobs and their homes because of their involvement in the cause), a course of action was launched that reached beyond the state constitution to the Constitution of the United States of America.

The case caught the attention of Thurgood Marshall, who

---

[32] *Brown v. Board of Education; Briggs v. Elliott; Davis v. County School Board; Gebhart v. Belton*, 347 U.S. 438 (1954).

was then general counsel to the N.A.A.C.P. and who later went on to become the first black Justice of the United States Supreme Court. He believed that separate but equal was morally wrong, that it was premised on the assumption that the Negro race was inferior, and that the practice of segregation was having a profound negative impact on the self-esteem of black children. Marshall, and the group around him, saw in this case, and in similar cases from other states, the opportunity to challenge the "separate but equal" doctrine that the Supreme Court of the United States had on seven previous occasions applied as the basis of the Fourteenth Amendment of the United States Constitution. However, they found themselves up against the strongly held belief of many in the black community that desegregation was impractical, that it would stir up discontent and racial strife, and that both whites and blacks were better off as separate solitudes as long as there could be equality of facilities. There were strongly held fears that the timing was not right, that the composition of the United States Supreme Court was not right, that the mood of the country was not right, and that an attempt at that time to challenge the separate but equal doctrine would set back the cause of civil rights in the United States for decades. Objectively speaking, there appeared to be nothing to indicate that the United States Supreme Court might be inclined to overrule itself, and to interpret the United States Constitution any differently than it had on the seven previous occasions.

The resulting decision of the United States Supreme Court to desegregate schools has been amply documented, analyzed and debated from practically every perspective, legal, sociological, ethical, demographic and political. However, for me, this film seemed to reach beyond the historical description, beyond the legal and political analysis, to tell a human story, a story about the people who brought the issue before the United States Supreme Court, and of the nine individuals on the Court who had to make the decision. Through a rather remarkable process, the Justices of the United States Supreme Court were able to see differently, not only the meaning of the Fourteenth Amendment, not only the nature of the constitutional process, but also their own roles as judges of a court that stands above the U.S. Congress as the final arbiter of the United States Constitution.

The appeal was argued on two occasions, before differently constituted benches of the Court. On both occasions the bench was largely dominated by what are often referred to as "conservative" judges - those who are dedicated to deciding cases within a fixed ambit of the Constitution, leaving it to the legislators to expand that ambit. For them, desegregation was a state legislative issue. They read the Fourteenth Amendment as giving to the legislature of South Carolina the exclusive authority to decide whether or not South Carolina schools should be desegregated. There was also on the Court a minority group of "civil libertarians," "judicial activists" who saw it as their role to use the United States Constitution to bring needed change to American society and its social attitudes. There was, understandably, deep division within the Supreme Court on the desegregation issue. While division was not unusual, there were two elements that made this situation different from most: first, there was a sense, even among the conservatives, that segregated schools were morally wrong; second, there was a sense that this was the most important case the Court would be called upon to decide in this century, and that a divided Court would send a mixed signal to the nation, fuelling social unrest on this fundamental issue.

After the first hearing, the only matter on which consensus could be reached was that the Court might benefit from further assistance on a troubling question: Was there any evidence that could demonstrate that the framers of the Fourteenth Amendment intended that it should prohibit segregation in primary and secondary schools? Counsel were asked to readdress the Court on that question. An intense research effort was mounted on both sides in an attempt to find, in the debates surrounding the adoption of the Fourteenth Amendment, something that might provide a clue.

The question that was put out for reargument reflected the conservative make-up of the Court. The majority of the Justices were bent on interpreting the Fourteenth Amendment in light of the intentions of those who had brought it into being. It was a view of a constitution fixed in time, bound by the perspectives of those who had brought it into being, however limited those perspectives might have been.

Between the time the case was ordered to be reheard and the date set for reargument, Chief Justice Vinson died and was replaced by Governor Earl Warren of California. Warren was essentially a politician, not a legal scholar. He had had no judicial experience, nor had he had much experience as a lawyer. His appointment, allegedly born in a political deal leading to the nomination of Dwight D. Eisenhower as the Republican presidential candidate, evoked a lot of scepticism, not only in legal and political circles, but within the Court itself.

And yet, what Chief Justice Warren achieved was truly

a miracle (as I have used the word in this book, i.e. a marked shift in perception). What we were shown in the film was the portrait of a man who came into touch with his intuitive feeling that segregation was not only morally wrong, but politically inappropriate for the United States of America at that point in its history. This was a nation that had fought a civil war over slavery, that had responded to the vision of Lincoln, and that held itself out to the world as a land of equal opportunity. However the words of the Fourteenth Amendment may have been understood by its framers, Chief Justice Warren saw the Justices of the Supreme Court in 1953 as being presented with the opportunity to give those words a meaning that was appropriate for the times, to see the United States Constitution as a source document, timeless, eternal, always contemporaneous, not frozen in the twilight of past controversies.

The film showed how Chief Justice Warren's vision opened the door for other Justices to express what they truly sensed - that segregation was morally wrong and that the Constitution was not to be used to suppress the conscience of the people. Warren was able to help each of the Justices look at the obstacles they had placed in the way of what they knew to be truth. He helped the brilliant legal scholar and judicial "conservative," Felix Frankfurter, to lay aside his strong commitment to the law as an interpretative process. He helped Mr. Justice Jackson to see beyond his opinion that this was purely a legislative matter. Warren helped others to see beyond the practical difficulties they perceived in implementing desegregation, and to celebrate the principle itself. Warren's vision led an essentially conservative court to the unanimous declaration that state practices of establishing segregated schools were unconstitutional.

It is not difficult for students of the law to become so engrossed in its logic and discipline as to overlook its human side. Watching this film was for me an opportunity to look differently at events I had looked at in the past mainly from a legal perspective. Here was the story of judges wrestling with their consciences, searching for a way to reconcile their understanding of how a legal and constitutional process was supposed to work, with what they knew in their hearts to be true. Each of them was given an opportunity to reexamine that role, and Chief Justice Warren was there to facilitate the process. The importance of the issue and the high profile of the case probably made it easier for the Justices to recognize and respond to the opportunity. And yet, essentially the same opportunity is presented to a judge each time a case comes before a court, i.e. an opportunity to see beyond appearances, an opportunity for healing.

As odd as this may sound, I believe that the role of judges is *not* to judge, remembering that I use the word "judgment" in this book in the sense of condemnation, not in the sense of impartial decision making. In my experience, most judges, like the rest of us, have a great deal of difficulty suppressing their instinct to judge, whether it be the motives or morals of the parties, the abilities of the lawyers, the integrity of the witnesses, or the policy underlying the positions put forth in argument. It is a habit we all pick up early in life, and it is nurtured by our culture, by our educational experiences and by the insecurities we have about our spirituality. There are lawyers who refuse to appear before certain judges, and there are clients whose cases are prejudiced because their lawyers take their cases before certain judges. That is a difficult allegation to prove, but there are many lawyers and judges I know who would agree with it, at least in part.

The only point I am making is that deciding cases is about more than the law, about more than the facts and about more than the application of law to facts. It is about relationships. It is about attachments, conflict and judgment, all of which tend to surface as the judge is called upon to address people, ideas, opinions, character, personalties and cultural differences in the course of making decisions. Those who like to judge our judges have to remember that they are human too. They have fears, anxieties and values that can influence their actions and decisions, just as they influence yours and mine. There is a helpful lesson from *A Course in Miracles* that is there to be remembered by all lawyers, parties or witnesses who may perceive themselves from time to time as being angrily berated by a judge: "I am never upset for the reason I think."[33] It applies as much to judges as to lawyers as to anyone else. What the lesson teaches is that there is always a more fundamental cause for our upsets, rooted in our insecurities about our spirituality and our inherent worth.

This is as true for others as it is for us. And so we can remind ourselves that we need never treat what may appear to be an attack by others as an attack *on us*. Forgiveness plays such a crucial part in healing because it helps us to see beyond the illusion of the attack we seem to encounter so regularly in our day to day experiences. It changes our perception of anger, both

---

[33] This is Lesson 5 in the Workbook, p. 8-9.

our own and someone else's, to a recognition of the call for love that underlies it. Forgiveness helps us to refrain from taking personally the angry outbursts of another; it enables us to function effectively in situations we might otherwise have seen as humiliating us. It heals the perception of separation. Healing comes as we look at the defences we have erected to protect ourselves from our illusory belief that we are being attacked by others, realizing that we can choose to dismantle them.

We tend to abdicate to judges much of the responsibility for sorting out the problems in our relationships with which we seem unable to deal. We rely on them to make many of our decisions for us, both as individuals and as a society. Not surprisingly, many of their decisions are met with disfavour, because they seem to conflict with values and attachments in which we may have a strong investment.

An example of the controversy that judicial decisions can raise is the recent ruling of the Supreme Court of Canada that the "rape shield" law is unconstitutional.[34] This was a provision of the Criminal Code designed to prevent evidence of a rape victim's prior sexual history to be presented before a court. The law was intended to encourage victims to come forth without fear of finding themselves "on trial" for their past conduct. The majority of the judges of the Supreme Court, in an opinion authored by Madam Justice McLaughlin, one of two women presently on the Court, held that a blanket exclusion of such evidence could be unfair to persons accused of sexual offences, denying them in some cases the ability to present evidence that is relevant to their defence. They felt the

---

[34] *R. v. Seaboyer*, decided on August 22, 1991.

relevance of the evidence, and the prejudicial effect of introducing it, should be considered by courts on a case by case basis, rather than having the matter determined by a rule that excluded the evidence in all cases.

People took to the streets to protest the decision, convinced as they were that the Court did not have its values properly ordered. Many, of both sexes, perceived the decision as an attack on women, or at least as showing blatant insensitivity to a serious dilemma facing many women. They saw it as giving support to male victimizers at the expense of female victims, not as an attempt to accommodate the values of fairness and protection in a particularly difficult policy area. As is usually the case when our expectations of the law seem to go unfulfilled, we seek refuge in blame and attack, rather than looking at the underlying cause of the conflict we are experiencing. I shall have more to say about this in Part IV when I discuss "Law and Social Policy."

There is no way to ensure that our judges will decide difficult cases with minds attuned to the Mind of God. Even if they did, our values and attachments might well lead us to reject the wisdom of Divine inspiration. After all, the controversy about school desegregation raged on long after the United States Supreme Court handed down its decision in the desegregation cases. And although I have used those cases as examples of the willingness of judges to see differently, to see beyond their personal values and attachments to a higher good or purpose, I have no doubt that many would disagree with my characterization of the cases in those terms.

Earlier in this book, I made some suggestions as to how, as a lawyer or as a client, I can implement my commitment to seeing law differently. Suppose, as a judge, I were to make a similar commitment. Are there ways in which that commitment could be honoured? I think that there are. As a judge, I can listen without having my judgment intrude upon what I am hearing. I can replace my moral indignation with forgiveness, by looking at my values and seeing beyond appearances. I can lay aside my desire to take control of the case that is being presented to me. I can try to understand the real essence of the conflict that underlies the problem with which I am presented. I can apply the law as best I can to respond to the problem as I understand it, realizing that this does not resolve the underlying conflict the parties are experiencing but may provide an environment that facilitates healing.

Above all, I can approach my duties in a state of love, not anger and resentment, realizing that this trial is part of my own healing process as well as that of the parties, lawyers, witnesses, and everyone else who has a role in it. I can be conscious of my spiritual connection with everyone and everything related to my job as the decision maker, recognizing that each person who is participating in the drama has the same opportunity to choose, in the moment, to dedicate their unique role to the expression of spiritual unity. In that regard, I can accept that my role as judge stands no higher in the sight of God than any other role. In each role lies the opportunity to forgive, to heal and be healed.

I do not offer the above as a suggestion that this is how judges *should* be doing their job. There is always the temptation to blame the conflict we experience in the legal system on the failure of someone else to do what it is we think they should be doing. That is true of life generally. We tend to think that things will get better for us if someone else changes what it is they are doing. How I would approach my role as judge may not be as someone else would. The same is true of my role as lawyer, or as client. The court provides, nonetheless, another arena, another opportunity in which the choice can be made to look in a different way at what it is we do. Many judges I know look hard to find contentment and a sense of fulfilment in what they do, and are deeply burdened by the seeming impossibility of many of the decisions they are called upon to make. Many are searching for a sense of purpose in what often appears to be an insane system of justice. To those who are open to finding a better way, I simply share my experience and my outlook for whatever meaning it may have for them in carrying out their function in the world.

# PART IV - CONTEXT

**There is another way of looking at the world.**

*A Course in Miracles*, Workbook, page 50.

## LAW AND SOCIAL POLICY

On a recent flight back to Ottawa, I read an article in the Yale Law Report[35] about Dean Guido Calabresi's first year Torts class at Yale Law School. Dean Calabresi is a much-honoured teacher and scholar at that institution. It brought back memories of my days in law schools, both as a student and as a teacher, learning and teaching about law as an instrument of social policy. How many first-year law students have sat completely bewildered as law professors explored how the meaning of law is shaped and reshaped by defining and redefining the social values that give law its content?

What struck me in reading the article was the sense of importance that legal education attaches to law and legal process. Law both reflects and secures moral, economic and cultural values and serves as the vehicle through which particular values dominate and control society. The interpretation to be placed on a law is that which best fulfils aspirations to achieve the values courts are persuaded are most important to our social fabric.

Our laws, it is clear, are more than the words we use to express them. Words are but symbols of symbols, twice removed from reality.[36] They symbolize the specific pictures we hold in our minds, which in turn are symbols for the deeper experiences we choose to have. It is at this experiential level

---

[35] Chris Goodrich, "The Dean Teaches Torts," Yale Law Report, Volume 37, No. 2, Spring 1991, p.2.

[36] This phrasing of this idea, which I have borrowed from page 51 of the Manual for Teachers of *A Course in Miracles*, appeals to me as a graphic way of expressing the relationship between law and language.

that values come into play. The words in which rules of law are expressed must be interpreted in order to be applied in specific situations, and lawyers and judges, who are trained in law, can only do this with the help of others who better understand than they do the social, political, economic, scientific and administrative context in which particular laws are expected to apply, and the values that relate to that context. Legal interpretation is thus an imprecise art, which is why students and laypersons alike, not to mention lawyers, experience so much frustration with the law. Sometimes it is like trying to read a rule book for a game, the conceptual framework and object of which you don't quite understand.

Much of the confusion stems from the fact that laws are made, applied and amended in a context no one wholly understands. Law is used to respond to problems that no one wholly understands. True, there are often extensive and sophisticated studies that predate the passage or amendment of a law, but however well they may be done, they are inevitably incomplete. Notwithstanding all the power of the human brain, and all the supplementary computing power afforded by modern technology, the context in which laws are enacted is necessarily incomplete. Intellectually and cognitively, we cannot know fully the dimensions of even the simplest problems we are called upon to solve.

Furthermore, many of our laws are enacted in an atmosphere of fear and anger. The parameters set down for studies that predate the passing of laws are often value-laden at the outset, and the laws that emerge respond only to limited aspects of the problem under study. Frequently there is emphasis on the need for action, or on the need to be *perceived* to be doing something, especially when the issue is seen to be a pressing matter of social concern. Consider, for example, the problem of family violence, which has become such a prominent focus for discussion in recent months. The Honourable Bertha Wilson, a recently retired Justice of the Supreme Court of Canada, who is currently heading up a Canadian Bar Association task force on gender equality, is one prominent and thoughtful Canadian who has spoken out publicly on this issue. She has stressed the need for "systemic remedies for what is undoubtedly a systemic problem."[37] In part, she has called upon Canadian society to look honestly and openly at the problem, which, as individuals and as a society, we have been unwilling to do. Beyond that, she has called for the need to recognize for women an equal status with men in the "outside world." "Violence ... is perpetuated by the fact that men do and women do not have power in our society." The solution is a form of power shift: "Men must come to acknowledge that the problem is really theirs; women are simply the victims of a system which has traditionally reflected male interests and favoured the male viewpoint. In the search for systemic remedies men must be willing to cast aside their own system for the simple reason that justice demands it."

Former Justice Wilson went on to acknowledge that the legal system has failed women, and that women perceive the system to be alienating and oppressive. She has called for change. Hers is a viewpoint that commands a lot of respect and

---

[37]  References here to the ideas of the Hon. Bertha Wilson are taken from a speech she delivered to the B'nai Brith Women of Canada, an excerpt from which was published in the Ottawa Citizen, May 29, 1991, at p. A15.

support. The part of me that feels anger and guilt at the thought of women being victimized by men and by a legal system dominated by men, wants to align myself with her. Another part of me, however, is uncomfortable at the thought of reinforcing the idea that women are victims, and that they are dependent on men changing their attitudes about them in order to experience their freedom. That thought seems disempowering.

And so I reach the point in this discussion that I reach in virtually all discussions about policy making on social issues; I sense that I am in the middle of an intellectual and emotional debate that has no real direction. That comment is not intended in any way to be critical of former Justice Wilson. It's that I feel that the intensity with which we often relate to issues of this sort tends to obscure the vision that is required to respond in a way that invites healing.

When I ask myself how Victor Hugo's metaphorical Bishop might have regarded the issue of family violence I see it somewhat differently. I see it as our being consumed, both men and women, by fear, by the belief that our worth is found outside ourselves, by the illusion that power is something outside us to be acquired, bartered, used and abused, and by our unwillingness to remember that we are spiritually connected beings. I see domestic violence as one of the manifestations of a crisis of spirituality in our culture. I do not see it as a legal or social policy issue that a government can deal with effectively without there being a shift in perspective of mind, and not just on the part of men. The responsibility begins with each one of us, individually, to re-examine our own sense of worth, and what we draw upon to determine and sustain that sense. Family violence is not just about the relationships between men and women. It is about our beliefs about ourselves. It is about our relationship with God.

In my opinion, forgiveness, not confrontation, is the "systemic remedy" that can bring about the needed attitudinal change. Forgiveness takes us beyond the belief in our victim-victimizer roles to the realization of our inherent equality. Those who are willing to forgive receive instant healing. Those who are not willing to forgive continue to experience conflict, and to see themselves as victims and victimizers caught up in the violence syndrome. From my vantage point, the "solution" to domestic violence begins in our openly looking at the situation, as men, women, children and youth, in a spirit of acknowledgement and forgiveness, sharing with all who are willing to receive it, the healing power of forgiveness.

Mine is not a position everyone will feel comfortable with. We live in a society that is so fearful of confronting its spirituality that it has purged many of its teachings of their spiritual content, a society that entrenches in its constitution freedom of thought, conscience and religion, and yet studiously strips its public institutions of spiritual reference points lest it be construed as fostering state religion. A spiritual approach to problem solving on public policy issues is not widely embraced, although it is now being brought back into our consciousness through our communications with aboriginal Canadians on constitutional and social issues.

Furthermore, mine is a position that, to many in our action-oriented society, may seem to do nothing. They will see the answer as lying in stiffer laws and law enforcement and affirmative action to strengthen the economic resources of women. Others, including the authors of a recent Canadian parliamentary report entitled *The War Against Women*, advocate more education in schools, better training of those in the justice system and more money for the helping groups, all of which undoubtedly would contribute to relieving the stress felt by those who see themselves as targets of violence. I view these as compatible and complementary approaches that can contribute positively to healing *if* they can be adopted without the anger, confrontation and acrimony that policy debates often generate, and if they can be carried out in a spirit of forgiveness. Only our unwillingness to forgive prevents us from looking for solutions in peace, which is the only context in which healing solutions come to light.

It is not so much *what* we do to deal with the problem of family violence, or any other social problem for that matter, as it is the spirit in which we do it. In my ideal world, all the laws would be made and applied by those who seek and receive spiritual guidance and who come from love and forgiveness, not from fear and anger. There is a great temptation to say that that is not *this* world; and yet, each of us who is involved with law and social policy has the opportunity and the choice to approach our function as a spiritual exercise, and thus to make it our world.

In emphasizing the *spirit* in which we do things, more so than the *form* which our policies, decisions and actions take, I am not suggesting that it is unimportant for lawyers and policy makers to be as competent as they can be in identifying the issues and impact associated with the application of a law in particular circumstances and in making adjustments to the law. An important part of advising a client or a government is to be able to outline competently the implications to be anticipated in respect of a particular decision, policy or course of action. A lawyer must be able to address in front of others, whether courts, administrative boards, government committees or other lawyers, in the most accurate way, how his or her client sees a given situation. In this respect, it may be necessary to expose errors of fact, errors of logic, errors in legal interpretation and errors in analysis that are colouring the view taken of a situation by another person or interest group or by the court. Those aspects of traditional "lawyering" are important, and my purpose is not to disparage them, or to criticize the training that leads to the development of those skills.

However, those skills alone are not enough to effect a healing of the conflict that underlies legal and social problems. Furthermore, there is a great temptation to use those skills in ways that exacerbate the conflict, rather than heal it. That, I think, was the essence of Chief Justice Burger's message in his 1984 address to the American Bar Association, referred to in my Introduction. It is a matter of perspective. Do I use my "lawyering" skills in the cause of peace and healing? Or do I use them to attack? My own choice is to look beyond the law, beyond social policy analysis, for the answers to the difficult issues that attract people to the law for solutions. It is not to disregard the law, or the social policy concerns that underlie it, but to treat both as a context for looking at more fundamental spiritual questions, such as: What is the real reason I am feeling upset? How can I find peace in this situation?

The law is a significant, pervasive presence in all our lives, and we are not able to ignore it, any more than we are able fully to understand it. And although, as a lawyer, I am committed to making an effort to understand what is not understandable, I find that my own emphasis has shifted. Rather than trying to better understand law in the hope of finding in it solutions to the world's and my clients' problems, I have come to accept it as part of a wider context in which to explore for spiritual truth.

I find it interesting that while I have been writing this book my son Geoffrey has made his own decision, uninfluenced by any conscious effort on my part, to choose law as a career. In light of that, I suggested that he read the article about Dean Calabresi's first year Torts class, wondering whether it would stimulate or dampen his interest in the study of law. Perhaps not surprisingly, he found the article extremely stimulating, as I would have at a corresponding stage. Looking back, I think that it has been an essential part of my development as a lawyer, and as a person, to understand the process by which laws are made, amended and enforced, and the deficiencies and shortcomings of that process. And so I have no reservations about the decision my son has made to study law. As I have suggested above, it is important to acquire a technical competence in the law, and a sense of how it relates to other dimensions of our social experience.

I also hope that Geoffrey will gain, early in his career, a greater appreciation than I did of the spiritual context in which law can be explored as a discipline. I am encouraged that ethical concerns are currently receiving greater emphasis in professional and business schools than formerly they were. It is important to expand the ethical horizons of those in the professions and business. It is equally important, in my view, to expose students to the spiritual foundations on which the principles of professional ethics rest.

Law can be seen in many ways: as a set of organizing principles for society, as a way of making a living, as a means of protecting and helping people, as a guarantee of freedom, or as an obstacle to freedom, to list just a few. We choose what meaning we wish to attach to the law, what role we want it to play for us. Life is about choices, and law is no less a matter of choice than anything else. My choice is to see it primarily as an opportunity for the healing of relationships within a broad social context. That context extends to the political battles that currently threaten to erode the constitutional underpinnings of Canadian society, and into the boardrooms of the nation. It extends from the intimacy of the family to every conceivable offshoot that brings people together in relationship. It extends to the relationship we have with the planet we inhabit. The context invites, indeed virtually calls out for, another way of looking at law and how it impacts on all these relationships. These are themes that are explored in the discussion that follows.

## THE CONSTITUTION

A constitution is a law that relates to our institutions of government. Among other things, it sets out how political power is divided between the executive and the legislative branches of government; how it is divided in Parliament and in Congress between those who proportionately represent the people and those who represent geographic interests; how power is divided between the federal government and the provinces or states; and how the judicial branch of government relates to the legislative and executive branches.

A constitution also defines rules that apply to the relationship between governments and individuals. In Canada, the *Canadian Charter of Rights and Freedoms* sets out various guarantees of freedom from interference from government. It enables us to make our own choices, good or bad, without being constrained by government, as long as they are not harmful to another person or to the public interest. The *Charter* bears many similarities to the much older *Bill of Rights*, which is part of the Constitution of the United States.

I have singled out constitutions for a brief discussion because it is a topic of much concern in Canada today. Canada is frequently described as being in a state of constitutional crisis. The Report of the *Citizens' Forum on Canada's Future*,[38]

---

[38] The *Citizens' Forum* was a diverse group of Canadian citizens who were appointed by the federal government in 1990 to investigate into Canada's future. The Forum went out to the people to meet them in community settings. According to the Forum, an estimated 315,000 citizens in some 13,000 groups discussed key issues such as Canada's identity and values, Quebec and unity, aboriginal peoples, official languages,

issued on June 27, 1991, reported strong feelings of anger, hatred and cynicism towards governments in general, and towards the federal government in particular. This was based on a series of public forums held across the country over several preceding months.

The crisis of values appears to arise from a diminishing awareness of and sensitivity to Canada's history, and a lack of clear, consistent vision as to its future. It seems as though the glue that has held the nation together for the past 125 years is drying up. There is talk of decentralization and possible separation of one or more provinces.

Strong pleas for constitutional reform are being heard from many quarters, as they have been for decades, but as yet there is no apparent consensus on what the content of that reform would or could be.[39] There are mixed feelings about the idea of a special status for Quebec, which is seen by many as necessary to preserve its cultural uniqueness, to say nothing of its willingness to remain a part of Canada. And while there is polite acceptance of the fact that the European colonialists years ago virtually destroyed the aboriginal culture of what is now Canada, there is no common understanding as to what can be done to help rectify decisions and actions that have been taken in later years to compound the original errors of our forefathers.

As well, Canada, being a country endowed with more than its share of resources and opportunities, has for some time

---

cultural diversity, the economy, leadership and democracy.

[39] The latest set of federal government proposals is presented in a document entitled *Shaping Canada's Future Together*, unveiled on September 24, 1991.

been a preferred destination of immigrants from all over the world, a trend that is escalating. That, coupled with a relatively low internal reproduction rate, affords a view of Canada as a growing multicultural society, a character that is alluded to in the *Canadian Charter of Rights and Freedoms*. As a result, any sociological process of value consensus is likely to become more difficult, which may compound the historical differences arising out of the French-English language issue, and our governments' inability or unwillingness to deal with the original inhabitants of the territory, namely the Indians and the Inuit.

The usual governmental response to pressure on the constitutional front has been to establish committees and commissions, to convene on-going conferences, to send task forces out into the field to consult and report and to seek consensus on a broad range of issues. Mountains of paper have been produced over time, years upon years of personal effort have been expended, and yet the debate goes on about substantially the same issues. I was personally involved in the one constitutional reform exercise that seemed to achieve some relative success, although I claim no special part in that "success." After months, actually years, of bitter acrimony and wrangling, nine of the provinces agreed on a deal that eventually resulted in the patriation of the Canadian Constitution from the United Kingdom to Canada (it had formerly been contained mainly in a British statute), the adoption and entrenchment of the *Charter*, certain modifications to the institutional structure of the federal government, and certain adjustments to the division of powers between Parliament and the provinces, notably giving the provinces more authority in respect of their natural resources.

In retrospect, the "success" of those constitutional

negotiations has probably added to the difficulties of the current crisis. Quebec, the only province that was not a part of that agreement, felt betrayed and insulted that there could be a deal made without its assent, and refused to acknowledge the agreement or the steps taken to implement it. It refused to participate in further discussions for a time, despite subsequent efforts to bring it into the fold. When the Prime Minister finally was able to bring Quebec and the other provinces to a somewhat imprecise agreement in the Meech Lake Accord, the succeeding months saw many of the provinces backing away from the deal. A last-ditch effort to save the Accord in a marathon conference in Ottawa resulted in a slightly modified agreement that proved not to be acceptable in the end to all governments. What directly killed the Accord was a filibuster by an Indian member of the Manitoba legislature, Elijah Harper, but the underlying reason was the lack of consensus among governments, and, more fundamentally, the lack of consensus among Canadian people about both the content of the Accord and the process by which it was reached.

As a result of all that, ultimatums have since been issued, suggested deadlines for the resolution of the crisis are being made and revised, and the nation has become consumed in the largest and most extensive and expensive flurry of constitutional activity yet seen in Canada. There are federal committees and commissions, provincial committees and commissions, native ones and private ones, all searching for answers. Some are approaching the issues from the standpoint of particular interests, and others from a larger, national perspective. Some people conceive of it as a political exercise; some see it as an intellectual and academic exercise. Scores of constitutional lawyers have been pouring over possible ways of reconfiguring the division of powers to reach an acceptable political compromise that would not emasculate the federal government. Political scientists and economists are looking at various proposals for change, to evaluate impact from the perspectives of their respective disciplines. Propagandists are hard at work shaping attitudes, working to convince people to believe that Canada must stick together or else terrible things will happen; or, conversely, depending on the point of view being promoted, that in separation lies new opportunity for prosperity.

I am asking myself: What is it all about? What is it all for? Are we looking for answers in the right places, or is this but a familiar replay of a seemingly endless and universal search for peace and stability through the manipulation of power and institutions? Are Canada's problems unique, or are we simply playing out our own form of the attraction to separation that is manifesting worldwide on the political stage? And is political separation any different from the sense of separation that we experience in our personal lives?

It must be curiously interesting to non-Canadians to watch a seemingly well-off country, in a non-violent way, struggle with discontent that would seem at first blush to be so much more comprehensible in countries that are less fortunate, materially speaking. There are important lessons for the world in the experience that is unfolding in Canada. Prosperity offers no refuge from the conflict that dominates political agendas. The so-called Canadian constitutional crisis seems nothing more nor less than another disconcerting illustration of the universal and ongoing crisis of the human personality.

The flurry of activity Canadians have embarked upon in response to the crisis may be perfectly useful. My role is not to judge, and my purpose is not to denigrate any of the efforts that have been undertaken to resolve the seeming impasse on the Canadian Constitution. My own thinking on this matter is that there are likely innumerable forms in which workable constitutional reform could be achieved. It is not the *form* of the Constitution that presents us with difficulty. Rather, it is the *content* that lies behind the form. That content is the set of thoughts or attitudes that give meaning to the form. Those thoughts can achieve high levels of sophistication, but a few examples in rather crude form should serve to illustrate what I am driving at. I hasten to add that these are not put out as my own, but rather as representative, thoughts or attitudes.

- Each province has unique interests that will be eroded if there are not express powers and protections given in the Constitution to guarantee that control over factors that affect them is in the hands of the provincial, not the federal, government.
- Conversely, what a provincial government may consider to be unique provincial interests are not really unique, because they have implications for interests located elsewhere in Canada. Therefore, to give powers and protection to a provincial government could put other Canadians at risk.
- It wouldn't be fair to give one provincial government something that the others don't have.
- A country with two languages doesn't make sense. Besides, I can never understand what Quebec is asking

for.

Ontario is the only province that Ottawa listens to because it has all the economic clout. The rest of us are treated in a patronizing way.

English Canadians don't like us, and they're rude and insulting.

French people are loud and obnoxious.

The Indians are out of their minds if they think they're going to get their land back. And why should we pay them for it? We won it fair and square.

- On second thought, maybe we didn't, so let's give them some money to make them happy.

Those are stereotypical thoughts, of course, and greatly oversimplified and exaggerated to be provocative. Truth to tell, however, they do, I believe, reflect attitudes that can be found in various parts of the country. My purpose in referring to them is only to illustrate different kinds of thoughts, all of which reflect varying degrees of distrust and prejudice, that can, if we choose to let them, affect the content we give to our Constitution. That content is not the noble rhetoric that politicians voice when called upon to explain the meaning of the words of the Constitution. The content is what we, as individual members of the society that makes up this nation, believe about ourselves, about one another, about our respective cultures, our institutions, our leaders, our past and our future. Individually and collectively, we are what we choose to be. The content of our Constitution can reflect our fears, our guilt, our distrust, our resentment, our sense of victimization and our sense of separateness. Or, it can reflect our love for each other, our spiritual unity, our respect for process, our commitment to peace, our gratitude and our willingness to share, not only amongst ourselves but with others in the world who are less fortunate.

How can we ensure that our Constitution will reflect love-based values, assuming that is the content that most of us would choose? One way is to express those values in the Constitution in a manner that touches the hearts of the people. A beautiful example can be found in the Report of the Special Joint Committee on a Renewed Canada, released on February 28, 1992. The Committee recommended that a statement of Canada's identity and values be included in a prominent place in the Constitution. In particular, it suggested the following preamble:

### PREAMBLE

We are the people of Canada,
drawn from the four winds of the earth,
a privileged people,
citizens of a sovereign state.

Trustees of a vast northern land,
we celebrate its beauty and grandeur.
Aboriginal peoples, immigrants,
French-speaking, English-speaking,
Canadians all,
we honour our roots and value our
diversity.

We affirm that our country
is founded upon principles that
acknowledge the supremacy of God,
the dignity of each person,
the importance of family,

and the value of community.

**We** recognize that we remain free
only when freedom is founded on
respect for moral and spiritual values,
and the rule of law
in the service of justice.

**We** cherish this free and united country,
its place within the family of nations,
and accepting the responsibilities
privileges bring,
we pledge to strengthen this land
as a home of peace, hope and goodwill.

However, to express such words in the Constitution is not enough. The content must find expression in the *process* of constitutional reform, and in the process through which we allow our constitution to unfold. The values that govern the process will, I believe, be reflected in what comes out of the process. I see in the process an opportunity for the participants, who are our proxies and our representatives, to demonstrate the love-based values expressed in the recommended preamble, and to create constitutional relationships and forms that reflect those values.

Whether the process be given to a "constituent assembly," as many have asked for, or to a selection of the political representatives we have elected to hold public office, each person to whom the function falls is presented with repeated opportunities to heal the conflict he or she experiences within such a process, and through that to bring healing to others. Each person is given many opportunities to forgive, to see beyond appearances, beyond their grievances, beyond their judgment and fear to the values that flow from our spiritual unity. Forgiveness is understanding that the interests of Quebecers are not different from those of Newfoundlanders. It is recognizing that our uniqueness in form, whether it be the distinct culture of Quebec or that of Newfoundland, does not threaten me; that it is the unique expression in form of our spiritual unity; that it is to be celebrated, not judged and feared.

In a practical vein, how is forgiveness brought to the table in constitutional negotiations? I think it is largely a matter of attitude. Forgiveness is parking my judgment at the door of the conference room, along with my past grievances, my defences, my anger, my resentment and all the other symbols of fear the process brings up for me. It is releasing attachments to outcomes that *I* think should arise from the process. It is recognizing that the process is about the Constitution of the whole of Canada, which reflects the interests of everyone around the table and everyone living in Canada, and that there are no special interests that are not equally the interests of everyone for whom the process exists. It is trusting my brothers and sisters around the table, and trusting in the process in which I have agreed to participate.

It is also about listening to what others are saying, without interrupting them, trying honestly to see the vision they are seeing, and discussing it with them and with others without fear, acrimony or defensiveness. It is keeping my peace in the face of extreme temptation at times to "let it all go."

There appears to be a tremendous amount of distrust and cynicism.felt by people today towards many institutions, but especially towards governments and politicians. It extends to all levels of government - federal, provincial, municipal and even subordinate forms of local government, like school boards. This attitude is not confined to Canada. Political systems are disintegrating all over the world. Less and less does the notion of territoriality make sense as the main organizing principle for government.

Communications technology has made borders largely irrelevant, and the instruments of modern warfare leave them impossible to defend. And because trade is now more than ever international and regional, political organization, which has always been heavily influenced by economics, tends to be more difficult to rationalize on narrow territorial principles. I mention this in passing only to suggest that it may be more difficult today than it once was to maintain the territorial organization of nations around secular values such as defence and economic prosperity. Nor do factors such as ethnicity or family dictate territorially based government when families, races and cultures are spread across the globe. Diversity of culture and religion within a territory reduce the potential for politically organizing a territory around those factors. Political organization on a territorial basis, apart from the practical requirements of local government, is beginning to look, at least in some sectors of the world including perhaps our own, more the result of habit and convenience than of functional requirement. This may well add to the difficulties of forging a national constitution in today's world, whether it be in what we know today as Canada, or elsewhere.

I see the constitutional process as presenting to all of us who call ourselves Canadians, but especially to those who have been called upon to participate directly in the process of change, opportunities of historic proportion to look at what relationship-building is really about. As heretical as it may seem, I do not think that the decisions as to whether or not Canada can or should remain an integrated whole, and, if so, on what terms, are as important as it is to look at the issues and to make the required decisions in a peaceful and forgiving spirit. Whatever constitutional form emerges from such a process cannot but help to serve us well.

I think as well that this is a lesson that is applicable world wide. It can lead to a new understanding about the constitutional and political process as a vehicle for expressing content in our relationships that is based in love and forgiveness, not acrimony, judgment and hatred. It is no different for Canada than it is for other federal political associations, whether it be the United States, the European Community or the new Commonwealth of Independent States. And it is no different in our larger political associations than it is in the seemingly lesser ones in which we carry out our daily lives. The process, and the content we express through process, are essentially the same, regardless of the form.

## BUSINESS

Many people would say that the really important decisions that affect the world are made not by politicians, not by lawyers or judges, but by people in business. Their decisions can control the local, national and international economy, make or break communities, inflict lasting damage on the natural environment, and dictate the shape of our culture. Business is a world of high finance, of cut-throat competition, of fine lines between success and failure, and of players who place winning above all else.

I am sure that everyone has heard those sweeping claims before, and doubtless there is an element of truth to what I have said, exaggerated though it may be. They raise interesting questions: How do businesspersons make decisions? How do they deal with the conflicts that arise when they become involved in legal disputes? Are they somehow different from the rest of us? Are they immune to the emotional strain that litigation can bring to the soul? Are their decisions made only on an economic basis? And where do spirituality and conscience fit in, or do they?

Many businesspersons work within corporations, which have legal lives of their own. In strict law, the dispute a corporation has with another corporation is that of the corporation, not of the directors and officers. Regardless of the conflict the directors and officers may personally experience in dealing with a dispute on behalf of the corporation, they are bound by the legal requirement to serve "the best interests of the corporation." Does this somehow limit their ability to deal with their own conflict? Is spiritual healing subordinated to secular interests? Can a corporate director serve the best interests of the corporation and serve God at the same time?

What *are* "the best interests of the corporation?" That has always proven to be a difficult question for lawyers and courts to answer. Typically, it has arisen in cases involving struggles for corporate control, often involving bids to take over the ownership of corporations. It can also be the subject of struggles between majority and minority shareholders. The directors, acting in furtherance of the majority shareholders who voted them into office, may be called to account for a decision the minority shareholders consider not to have been made in the best interests of the corporation.

Some courts have attempted to set firm rules about what can and cannot be done in the best interests of the corporation, particularly when it comes to issuing and selling shares. Other courts have been more deferential towards the decisions the directors make, as long as they have not breached any fiduciary duty, that is, they have not made decisions that benefit themselves personally at the expense of the corporation.

In serving the best interests of the corporation, corporate directors often have to face issues that have legal dimensions. They may be required to decide on the firing of senior officers, on whether or not to evict a tenant, on the nature and scope of corporate compliance with environmental and occupational safety rules and regulations, on whether to take enforcement initiatives in respect of contractual disagreements with other parties, or on how to implement pay equity and human rights legislation. On many of these issues, which I have picked at random, the law will not be wholly determinative and the decision will reflect other factors. Usually it will be heavily influenced by fiscal considerations. Many directors feel strongly that their roles as corporate decision makers are very much constrained by the need to maximize profits for the shareholders.

Often, however, there will be competing interests that surface, for example those of employees whose jobs may be affected by a decision. Sometimes a whole community may be threatened, for example where a decision to downsize or sell the activities of a major corporation is made. Sometimes a decision will affect the ecology and the social and recreational patterns that depend upon it. Does the law require the director to ignore those considerations and to respond exclusively to the financial advantages to the owners of the corporation, the shareholders? And how are the short term interests of the corporation to be measured against its longer term interests? These latter interests may be more compatible than the former with the broad social interests that are affected by the decision.

Questions along these lines were raised at a recent gathering of the Harvard Business School Alumni in Ottawa by Peter Lougheed, formerly Premier of Alberta and now a director of many influential private sector corporations.[40] At that same gathering I heard Professor Thomas Piper, Associate Dean for Educational Programs at the Harvard Business School, give a thoughtful and compelling call for more attention to ethics in corporate governance. He outlined the approach taken at his school to integrating ethical values into the curriculum. Although his talk was not expressed in spiritual terms, there was spiritual content in his approach. He was looking for answers

---

[40]    I attended this gathering at the Chateau Laurier Hotel in Ottawa on June 18, 1991.

that reflected more than the corporate balance sheet.

Because the business world is usually portrayed to be so deeply committed to the pursuit of material gain, it is easy to recoil from the thought of even broaching the subject of spiritual decision making as an approach to resolving conflict in that world. And yet, it seems to me that it is as relevant an approach there as elsewhere. To put the proposition more strongly, I would like to turn around a question I raised earlier in this discussion by asking it this way: Can a corporate director serve the best interests of the corporation *without* serving God? In view of the myriad factors that bear upon anyone's "best interests," whether it be a human or a fictional legal person, how can one ever know what those best interests are? How many examples come to mind of seemingly well-planned business ventures that turned into economic catastrophes, whether it be the ill-fated "Edsel" project of the Ford Motor Company, a memory of my youth, or the more recent disastrous foray of the Campeau Corporation into the retail sales markets of the United States? And how many corporations have found themselves caught in the middle of expansion plans as the economy takes a sudden downturn?

"I do not perceive my own best interests."[41]

What that brief offering of spiritual insight suggests to me is that deciding what my own or my corporation's best interests are in any situation comes down to a blend of analysis and intuition. And there is nothing that I see in the legal test

---

[41]   *A Course in Miracles*, Workbook, Lesson 24.

that would prevent those who believe that our abilities to reason and discern are markedly enhanced when we bring ourselves into touch with the peace that is within us, from drawing upon spiritual guidance in deciding what is, and what is not, in the corporation's best interests.

It is my view that one *cannot* serve the best interests of the corporation without serving God. Although I appreciate that the legal test would never be expressed in that way, I nonetheless find it interesting to see the law moving increasingly towards the recognition of the personal responsibility of directors for decisions that are made in the name of the corporation. The interests of corporations are being drawn closer into line with the interests of the communities in which they operate, and directors are being forced to reexamine their roles in a larger social context. Corporate directors may find it helpful to stretch their horizons to find a little willingness to "see differently," i.e. to see that in spiritual terms the interests of the corporation cannot be separate from God.

Some are already in touch with that idea. I have a friend, a skilful and successful businessman, who has told me that he no longer makes any important business decision without first consulting God. I can sense in his process a detachment from the secular trappings of the problem with which he is dealing in order to allow for spiritual guidance to come through. Sometime earlier, before either of us were as aware as we have since become of the meaning and importance of integrating our spirituality into every facet of our lives, I had watched this same friend become frustrated and disillusioned while defending a lawsuit brought against his company, the merits of which I had thought at the time were highly dubious. It had been his first major legal wrangle, and he had been drawn into it with some reservation but with a strong sense of the rightness of his position. It turned out to be a costly and difficult experience, and one he had not been prepared for. Although I did not act as his lawyer in the matter, we did discuss it from time to time. I realize now that I did nothing to help him appreciate the process he was entering into, and instead reacted in a traditional lawyerly way whenever we spoke about it. In the end, he made the choice to settle on terms that he was unhappy with, feeling it was necessary to do so in order to protect the larger interests of his company. I take some comfort in the fact that he now speaks with God before he speaks to me or to other lawyers about such matters, although I think that I too have since learned to look beyond my intellect and my emotions when called upon to address his questions.

The example I have just given reinforces what I have been told by those who are better informed than I that many businesspersons, perhaps even more so than other legal consumers, are looking for a better way of dealing with conflict than the legal system presently offers. And although I realize that for many the emphasis is more on efficiency than on spirituality, I have the impression that many businesspersons have a much deeper commitment to spiritual values than is commonly accepted. This is in spite of the fact that the business culture, as does the legal culture, tempts us to erect barriers behind which we can hide our spirituality, not only from others but often from ourselves.

The law certainly does not prevent businesspersons, any more than anyone else, from exploring decisions from a loving rather than a fearful perspective. Their decisions are as much opportunities for healing as any of the decisions referred to elsewhere in this book. The application of the laws that regulate business, which include commercial and corporate law as well as the many specific laws that regulate the myriad activities in which businesspersons are active, present as many opportunities for healing as do other laws. They are laws that govern and affect relationships, as much as any laws do; and the conflicts that emerge among businesspersons are as much about relationships as are those that emerge among politicians, or within families, or in the workplace or on the highways. The forms may be different, but the content is the same. It is about fear, control, attack and attachments.

I cannot claim to have had as much experience of how law is integrated and applied in the world of business as I have had in seeing how law relates to government. I would like, however, to share one small incident surrounding the settlement of a contractual dispute, one which may serve to illustrate the healing approach I am describing in this book. My friend and client Ralph, along with a colleague, had worked on a consulting project for a large international network marketing company based in the United States. The work had come out of informal discussions Ralph had had with the president of the company, but which had not been put in writing, either in a letter or a more formal document. Ralph, perhaps rightly and perhaps wrongly, assumed that the work had been authorized and went ahead and prepared a consultant's report. He is that sort of person, eager to get at it and get the job done. When he submitted the report, along with his account for payment, to the head of the company's Canadian operations, he was told that the study had not been authorized and that he could not be paid for his work. There was no question that the study had been competently done. It had simply not been ordered.

Inquiries by Ralph into the situation soon revealed that there was a general atmosphere of conflict and insecurity in the management levels underneath the president, particularly in relation to the Canadian operations of the company. When Ralph approached the president directly about the difficulty he was having in collecting payment for his work, the president seemed to support the position taken by his management team. The president told Ralph that it was his recollection that their earlier discussion had been preliminary and had been subject to further thought and confirmation. It was Ralph's impression that the problem had less to do with himself than it did with strained relations within the company. Nonetheless, I advised Ralph, from a legal standpoint, that he had no more than a possible case and that a court might easily come to the conclusion that he had "jumped the gun."

Ralph is a spiritual person and did not seem to be upset at what I told him. He said he wanted to think about it before deciding what to do. The next day he came back to me with a proposal. He wanted me, as a lawyer, to send under my signature to the president of the company a letter along the lines of one he had drafted. He asked me to revise the letter in whatever way suited my style for legal letters of this sort, but he wanted the letter to do two things: first, he wanted it to state the circumstances as he saw them, without acrimony, grievances, judgment, accusations or any of the hyperbole that so often finds its way into such letters to intimidate the recipient or to serve as a negotiating position. Second, he wanted the letter to reflect his trust in the president to do what was just, without stating Ralph's own opinion about what that might involve. I think Ralph had truly let go of all stake in the outcome and trusted that he would be taken care of in the appropriate manner.

I drafted the letter in accordance with my instructions and ended with the message that my client had made a complete abdication of the power of decision on the issue and had declared his acceptance, in advance, of whatever the president considered to be fair.

I received by return mail a letter from the president of the company thanking me for my letter and commenting, in what I took to be a positive way, that it was the most unusual letter he had ever received from a lawyer. With his letter he enclosed a cheque for eight thousand dollars, which was exactly half the amount Ralph had submitted as his account. He indicated that he had accepted the mandate we had given him, and that this was the amount he believed was fair under the circumstances.

There was not a large amount at stake, and it is perhaps an anecdote of relatively small proportions, quantitatively speaking. Nonetheless, I have always attached a lot of significance to it. I was truly impressed at how the players had carried out their roles. There was release, forgiveness, trust and acceptance on Ralph's part; he received his money in the spirit of the process he had initiated. And there was full and honest acceptance by the president of the role that had been asked of him. I truly believe that both of them walked away from the disagreement without any residue of conflict, both feeling that they had experienced a healing.

That incident was an awakening for me as well. It was then that I received my first inkling that the spiritual principles of which I was just becoming aware actually held out the promise of practical application in the world. The more I have worked with the principles since then, and the more I have opened myself to seeing how they apply in different areas of my experience, the more I see that in every walk of life the essential problem is the same, and the solution is the same. It is the willingness to forgive and to receive the healing that forgiveness brings. It is the willingness to look beyond appearances, to relinquish grievances and judgment, and to accept responsibility for our choices, whatever they may be, in every situation. Being active in the world of business does not, any more so than being active in the world of law or government, mean giving up our natural state of happiness, which we experience when we are in touch with our Source in whatever we do and in making the decisions we are called upon to make in that context.

## THE ENVIRONMENT

There is no hotter topic today than the environment! Stories about global warming, extinction of species, destruction of rain forests, pollution of lakes, rivers and oceans, air pollution, waste management, disposal of nuclear waste, chemical spills, recycling, and on and on, fill the media. People are highly sensitive to the problems, the issues and the lack of immediate solutions. They are also sensitive to the idea that each person plays a part both in the problems and in the solutions. More and more people are becoming aware of the inter-relationships amongst all elements of the biosphere, and of the importance of balance and harmony. There is, on the physical plane, a growing recognition of what, on the spiritual plane, I have referred to in this book as our spiritual unity, our interconnectedness. Interestingly, it seems easier for many people to accept that the *actions* they take individually affect the harmony of the *physical* world than it is for them to accept that *how they think* as individuals affects the harmony of the *spiritual* whole, and ultimately is reflected on the physical plane. Perhaps it is because we have come to rely on what we see with our eyes more than what we feel in our hearts.

I believe that our ability to address in a creative way our growing concerns about the environment is enhanced by our attentiveness to our spiritual health and well being. If, as I believe, the physical world is but a mirror of our thoughts about our spiritual state, then my understanding of the inter-relationships of all its elements not only helps me to appreciate our spiritual interconnectedness; it also underscores the importance of addressing environmental issues at the spiritual level as well as at the physical. Becoming "green," for me, entails an expression of my spirituality.

There is an increasing willingness today to look at the physical world and at our relationships with it differently than we did twenty-five years ago, in the early days of the movement towards ecological sensitivity and responsibility. There is a growing commitment to the notion of trust: the physical world is a gift to be enjoyed, preserved, shared and passed on. To my mind, that expresses a spiritual commitment, although I suspect that many who subscribe to that notion might not think about it or acknowledge it in those terms. There is also the recognition that the laws of nature, which we see as governing the harmonious flow of the world's energy, are not enough to sustain it. Mankind is capable of destroying the world if self-restraint is not practiced. And so, many "laws of the world" have been put in place to supplement and assist the operation of the laws of nature.

As is the case with other laws of the world, these laws not only address conflict but are seen to generate conflict as well. Environmental laws have become increasingly interventionist to the point that the cost of compliance has begun to eat away at our ability as a society and as citizens to enjoy the standard of living we have become accustomed to.[42] Many of

---

[42] A recent story in the Ottawa Citizen (Jan. 24,1992) reported the reactions of the Alberta government to the decision of the Supreme Court of Canada given on the previous day in a case involving the Oldman River dam project in that province. The Court (8-1) ruled that the project (already completed) should not have proceeded without a federal environmental impact assessment. The decision, which has also now served to heighten public awareness of the confusion that exists as to the

the benefits we took for granted as a society, at the expense of the environment, are no longer available to us. This tends to colour our understanding of the role of these laws. Rather than seeing them as efforts to facilitate our relationships with each other and with the planet and attempting to work with them in that spirit, we can become distracted by our sense of how they impact on what we see as our separate interests. Thus, there are some who regard environmental laws, and their requirements for environmental impact assessments, product development standards and land use requirements, as overly stringent and demanding. In some cases compliance is either evaded, avoided or performed grudgingly.

More and more, however, I sense a greater understanding of the importance of complying with these laws, and a corresponding willingness to comply. Undoubtedly, the threat of large fines contributes to this willingness, but I think there are more substantial reasons that are influencing today's attitudes. They are related to the growing awareness of the scope of the environmental context, of which I spoke in my introductory observations about this topic.

Conflict is also apparent in the ranks of the regulators, who sometimes see themselves pitted as adversaries against those who do not measure up to their environmental standards. Often they are perceived as adversaries by those who are made subject

---

division of constitutional authority over environmental issues as between the provinces and the federal government, may have the effect, it was suggested, of costing Canadians billions of dollars because of its impact on other planned projects. It is an illustration of the high priority that is now being given in our laws to environmental harmony.

by law to the regulatory regime. Even though the regulators and the regulated often share a broad common goal to preserve the global trust, different perceptions of the extent and nature of their respective roles can lead to disputes over implementation and compliance. The significant amounts of money that are at stake, both in fines and in civil damages, tend to entrench these adversarial perspectives.

Conflict can be seen as well in the growing segment of society that has assumed a self-imposed responsibility to enforce environmental standards. This is evident both in the form of group action and individual action. There are growing numbers who have formed strong attachments to the cause of the environment, and who see themselves as activists in support of the cause. Frequently, anger and resentment are directed towards those who are perceived not to be complying with our laws. Judgment manifests in calls for the vigorous enforcement of our laws in efforts to "attack" those who transgress them. There are demonstrations and slogans, and sometimes even physical responses taken against environmental polluters.[43] There are psychological pressures (guilt sensitizing) exerted to

---

[43] One can think of many examples. There have been several verbal and physical confrontations reported in the press over the years arising out of efforts undertaken by private citizens and groups to halt the killing of seals and other animals for the fur trade. That illusion is seen by many people to be less acceptable than the killing that occurs in the slaughterhouses of the world to support the massive food and leather goods industry. One might ask whether the hate that is directed towards the perceived wrongdoers belies the "love" that is said to precipitate it. The fervour with which we tend to identify with causes can block the inner harmony that is so important to healing.

influence compliance, as well as more neutral educational efforts that are designed and undertaken to work towards changing people's attitudes. In respect of many issues, the atmosphere has become quite emotionally charged.

In view of the conflict that environmental issues seem to attract, it may be helpful to consider briefly what these environmental laws represent, over and beyond their apparent role in protecting our life forces from abuse and exploitation, and how we can relate to them in ways that will reduce conflict and work towards not only the healing of the planet but our inner healing as well. I detect a certain irony in the fact that conflict should arise around the application and enforcement of our laws relating to the environment. For reasons I have expressed, I look upon environmental laws, more so than most laws, as teaching us the importance of harmony and as illustrating on the physical plane the spiritual principle of giving and receiving.[44] In few areas of the law is non-compliance so visibly counterproductive. Because the elements of the physical world are used and enjoyed by all of us, pollution is a

---

[44] The idea that giving and receiving are the same is a spiritual principle that recognizes abundance and the continuous extension of love from our Source. As we "give love away" to others, it flows through us. To experience that flow, we must share love, not try to "hang onto" it. Similarly, when we "forgive," we are extending love, which is why forgiveness is the gift that we give. "Healing" is the contemporaneous gift we *receive* as we forgive. These words, imprecise though they necessarily are, express shades of the same idea of interrelatedness that is reflected in the physical universe when we are sensitive to the flow of life and the harmony of nature. The care that we give to the earth is returned to us as an expression of abundance.

detrimental impact we can all see and feel in our lives. Conversely, compliance is rewarded with benefits that are becoming easier and easier to appreciate.

It is also easier in the field of environmental law than it is in many areas of law to see the role of the lawyer as facilitator. Environmental planning, environmental audits and environmental hearings all involve the mastery of a lot of difficult information, and entail cooperation with engineers, planners, consultants and regulators of various kinds. It is an area in which coordination and negotiation is vital. When disputes arise, it is important to look at options other than litigation. Regardless of the form in which the issue arises, I see it as the lawyer's role to find for the client the most expeditious and efficient way of resolving it. Here again, the significant levels of financial risk that our laws are seen to impose on those who may be associated in various ways with environmental transgressions, and the persistent fears we entertain about loss and lack, are major obstacles we place in the way of peace and healing.

To be willing to work towards releasing the conflict that we feel in relation to environmental issues and the use of environmental law is to reinforce our commitment to the environmental harmony that these laws are designed to sustain. The conflict we harbour in our minds works against our goals of harmony in the physical world. I see the blending of the physical and spiritual perspectives on the environment as having a synergistic effect. My attentiveness to the harmony of the physical world teaches me the importance of my attentiveness to my spirituality. And my attentiveness to my spirituality allows me to experience a more harmonious world. Although I see that principle as applying universally within our experience, not just in the environmental context, there is almost a symbolic importance that attends the goal of peacefully resolving our conflict about environmental issues. If we cannot resolve our environmental conflicts in the spirit of peace and harmony, how can we resolve conflict peacefully where the connection between our physical and spiritual perspectives is less obvious?

The environmental issues we face, and the laws we put in place to deal with them, have much to teach us about our spirituality. Seeing law differently in this context is to appreciate this teaching function and to accept the importance of finding our own inner harmony as we deal with our conflict. It is to extend the peace we find within ourselves to others with whom we are relating as we work through our seeming disputes and disagreements about implementation and compliance. I cannot resist the urge to add my own slogan to the many that have surfaced of late to capture the energy of the environmental movement: "When you start to see red, think *green*."[45] The benefits of harmonious thinking are felt not only by yourself and those with whom you are relating directly; they are felt by the entire world.

---

[45] I am told that in spiritual symbolism green is often seen as a colour of healing, which reinforces the link I have made between environmental harmony and inner healing.

## THE FAMILY

I want to conclude this discussion of context by touching on a few aspects of law as it relates to the family. Our families generally provide our closest relationships. Not only are we bound to our spouses, parents and children by bonds of love and affection, the law defines a mandatory economic link and standard of care. Spouses have mutual expectations of and responsibility for support and property sharing. As well, parents must support their children until they achieve prescribed levels of independence. In some legal jurisdictions children are liable to support their elderly parents. Quite apart from laws relating to economic support, family protection laws are there to ensure that standards of care and nurturing are maintained within families, and to ensure that the custodial arrangements for children are in their "best interests."

A strong emphasis on spousal and children's rights tends to diminish any reinforcement the law might otherwise give to the notion of the family as a spiritual unit. The "family unit" in law is made up of separate legal rights and interests, and those interests are entitled to and are often required to have separate representation in the legal process. Any presumptions that the law might at one time have entertained that spouses and parents were responsible and competent to make decisions in the best interests of the family and its members have either disappeared or been modified as the dynamics of the family have undergone dramatic changes over the last half century, and particularly over the last quarter century.

It has become more and more evident in recent years that there is a long history of intra-family violence, abuse and neglect in our culture. I alluded to this earlier in this Part. One can hardly read a single edition of any newspaper without coming across at least one story of seemingly incomprehensible abuse. And frequently the incidents that are reported reach back to events that occurred years ago. As a result, there are escalating demands for more intrusive and more effective legal measures to regulate and resolve family conflict, in the interests of preserving the safety and welfare of family members, particularly of wives and young children. Provincial and municipal social services departments are consuming more and more public money in programs that attempt to ensure that men, women and children can live together in relationship without killing, maiming or psychologically destroying one another.

It is crucial to look at this, because unhappiness in our family relationships spills out into virtually all other relationships. We have all had the experience of how difficult it is to be happy when we face conflict at home. At the same time, difficulties in other relationships in our lives, whether it be with friends, employers or fellow employees, or discontent with the nature of our work or our financial situations, tend to affect our family relationships. The cause and effect interplay among these factors is hard to track, and perhaps all we can do is observe the downward spiral. Most statistical surveys report that, for whatever reason, one in three marriages ends in divorce. More troubling is the fact that the courts are dealing every day with child protection cases and with criminal dockets that invariably include many family related offences. My own attribution of cause for this phenomenon to the erroneous beliefs we hold about ourselves, to our misguided quest for our worth outside ourselves, and ultimately to our unwillingness to resolve our relationships with God, is a subject I have already touched upon elsewhere in this Part and in other Parts of this book, and I will not pursue it further here.

Family conflict is perhaps the most difficult, and yet in many respects the most important, area in which to put into play the principles and attitudes I write about in this book. Many of those who practice law in this field will say it simply cannot be done: emotions run too high; there is an eagerness to use the law to attack one another and to bring about the loss of esteem that every player in the drama feels when family relationships break down. It is much easier, I have no doubt, for many practitioners in this field to play into the hands of fear and guilt, to empathize with the victim roles of their clients, and to reinforce and support the strong feelings of separation that the parties usually feel, than to focus on healing. It is easier to blame the other party, the other party's lawyer, and any other person or object upon which fear and anger can be projected, than to see the conflict in the light of truth.

Most lawyers I know place family law at the bottom of their list of preferred areas of practice. It is generally regarded as a battleground to avoid. Those who practice in this area seem to survive by distancing themselves as much as possible from the *causes* of the problems they deal with, using the symptoms or effects as grounds for legal claims and court applications made in support of their clients' interests. My own limited experience in family practice, at the very outset of my career, seemed at the time to offer me reasons for choosing a career in law teaching rather than practicing in this field. I taught family law for several years, and went on to do studies and to prepare legislation to reform several areas of family law, in particular property, support, child welfare, custody and adoption. Throughout that phase of my career I maintained a sharp focus on the need to enhance rights, to improve their enforcement, and to ensure adequate legal representation of all parties, especially children, as reluctant as I had been to join forces with the lawyers in the trenches who held themselves available to deliver those services to the public.

One of the most persistent criticisms of how the law relates to family conflict is that it places too much emphasis on the use of the adversary process. In part that is a by-product of the increasing emphasis on rights. Many lawyers think of the courts as the appropriate adjudicators of any question involving rights. Steps have been taken to try to offset the tendency of lawyers to focus on traditional legal process, by requiring that other processes be explored as ways of resolving disputes. In divorce, for example, lawyers are obliged by law to satisfy themselves that the parties have explored possibilities for reconciliation, and to advise their clients of counselling opportunities that are available. Some lawyers take that more seriously than others. Many clients will either have explored those options already, or will have discarded counselling as a practicable approach, given their circumstances.

More significant, perhaps, is the fact that family courts have integrated counselling, mediation and other support services into their regular processes. Undoubtedly these services help in some cases to blunt the sting of the adversary process. Family conflict is an area in which mediation is frequently advocated as a way of expediting the resolution of legal problems, and many lawyers, psychologists and family counsellors have established a substantial practice in mediation, some within the family court system and some outside it. The mediation process has its detractors, however, especially in those who point out how easy it is for the parties to compromise their legal rights when they enter this process.

I have my own reservations about mediation, but for a different reason. The process is fine. It is less formal than litigation, and helps keep the parties in communication with one another. There is sometimes a tendency, however, to centre on the *form* of the process and not on its *content*. To my mind mediation is more likely to result in healing if it is approached as a spiritual process, than it is if approached simply as a technology. I see mediation, like all other processes, as essentially neutral. It is only when spiritual content flows through the process that it takes on the role of a healing agent.

I suspect that many lawyers, and many clients for that matter, will have difficulty identifying with healing as the predominant goal in a family dispute. And those who do identify with the goal will find it very difficult at times to pursue. It seems to me to be of utmost importance for lawyers, if they are committed to healing, to work at maintaining the integrity of their own processes when assisting their clients to come to grips with the property settlements, support and child custody issues that attend the breakdown of marriage. The perspective on conflict I shared in Part I of this book, and the techniques I described under the heading "Lawyers and Clients" in Part III, offer ways to keep lawyers on track as facilitators of conflict resolution, not exacerbators of conflict. Looking upon themselves as facilitators, as healers, they will recognize that litigation is only one process out of many options that may be available to serve their clients. The ethical rules of conduct for lawyers, at least in Ontario where I practice, call upon lawyers to encourage voluntary settlements, and to assist their clients to work towards these settlements. In large part this entails an understanding of the conflict their clients are experiencing, and helping them to come to grips with it in the process of negotiating settlements or undergoing mediation through an independent mediator.

Let me move now to a different point, which I shall make in the context of the family although it applies equally in every context in which law operates. In part, seeing law as an opportunity for healing involves recognizing that most of the laws of the world are made and applied in response to fear, and as such serve to reinforce our beliefs about separation, not spiritual unity. This can be disconcerting for those who make the effort to look at the world from a spiritual perspective, and find themselves frustrated by the law. A spiritually oriented friend of mine, Tom, whom I introduced in Part III, recently complained to me about the fact that his wife had been required by a lending institution to seek separate legal advice before guaranteeing a business loan he was negotiating. He told me that his wife implicitly trusted him, supported him in his business, and felt entirely secure in discussing the matter with "their" lawyer. She felt uncomfortable and resentful about having to seek separate "independent" advice from "her" lawyer, to whom she was referred by "their" lawyer to give her advice on this single occasion.

I explained to Tom how this rule had evolved to protect wives from being exploited by dominating husbands, and I offered that I had on occasion either performed that role, or made similar arrangements for a spouse to be counselled independently. Still, I had to agree with Tom that this law is fear-based in its approach, and could be seen as obstructing the freedom of spouses to choose to arrange their affairs in a mode of spiritual unity, rather than one of conflict and separation. The underlying legal principle is that a lawyer cannot ethically represent two separate interests that are potentially in conflict. Because the law recognizes the separate interests of the spouses a lawyer cannot act for both of them. A lawyer can act as mediator as *between* spouses, but not as a lawyer *to* both.

There are, nonetheless, occasions when I have met with spouses together, on the clear understanding that I was not acting for either one of them, individually, but rather to facilitate a process they had chosen to undergo together. I think it is important that people have this option, if they have consciously chosen to look beyond the separateness the law attributes to their interests and to affirm their spiritual interconnectedness. In such circumstances I feel committed to facilitate whatever legal process may be involved. In doing this, I give them as clear an explanation as I can of what the law entitles them to individually, ensuring that both are committed to the process they have chosen. Even then, it may be impossible to accomplish such a process entirely on their own, as, for example, when a third party lender insists on independent advice for a spouse, or where the arrangement involves the consideration of the interests of children.

The fact that the law does not always measure up to the standards we might demand of it in a perfect world is a source of frustration for many people. All I can suggest is that they look at that frustration and see it as simply another opportunity to deal with the conflict it brings up for them. Often there is a way of coping with the seeming obstacles the law presents, if lawyers are prepared to lay aside their preconceptions and prejudices about what clients want to accomplish and about how the law should work, and to open themselves to finding, together with their clients, a way to deal with situations innovatively.

Where a law takes the form of a prohibition, the fact that it appears to be based upon a fearful view of the world hardly justifies disobeying it. If that were the case, most of the laws that are designed to protect society from possible harm would not be enforceable. However, laws are often expressed in ways that do not prohibit action, or require any mandatory action to be taken. The law may simply evince a policy or preference that people should act in a certain way, without actually directing that they do. Many laws are designed to induce or to influence behaviour, rather than to control it outright. In those cases, one is left with the choice to conform with the policy of the law, or not to.

For example, many of our laws in relation to child welfare, education and health are expressed in broad standards that allow considerable scope for individual decision making. For example, the law does not usually require parents to educate their children at specific institutions, or at any institution, as long as certain standards are met. Although the policy of the law is strongly directed towards institutional education, it recognizes other educational options. Similarly, parents are not specifically required by law to use conventional medical facilities and methods, even though the policy underlying the law may influence parents in that direction. Immunization laws, for example, usually contain exceptions that will accommodate those who take a different view of health and disease. Even the law that requires independent financial advice to be given to a spouse who guarantees a loan is not, strictly speaking, mandatory, in the sense that a lender is not specifically required to insist that advice be obtained. There is simply a risk that the guarantee will not be enforceable without independent advice having been given.

In the normal course, most people are inclined to take the cautious approach and to bow to the influence of the law. This is understandable; after all, the law is being used as an instrument of social policy to achieve that result. It is important, nonetheless, to recognize that you have a choice in any situation in which the law leads you, but does not direct you, to take a course of action with which you do not feel comfortable. You are free in these situations to follow your instinct to listen to the voice of love, rather than surrender to the voice of fear. In that regard, I want to conclude this discussion by sharing briefly a personal experience that demonstrated to Barbara and me how much joy can result when we close our ears to the voices of fear, reinforced though they may be in the laws, practices and conventional wisdom of our society, and when we trust instead to follow the intuitive guidance we know in our hearts to be true.

One of the burning issues in recent years in the law of adoption has been the extent to which the law should facilitate, or conversely preclude, access to information about the identity of the birthmother of adopted children. The laws of some legal jurisdictions impose strict regulation of this matter, driven as they are by concerns about privacy, emotional trauma and family conflict. There is a great deal of fear that has been expressed about what might happen if people, particularly young people, were given access to identifying information about adoptions. Many people feel closely aligned to the policy reflected in such laws. For them, the fear it addresses may appear to be very real. Complying with the policy of the law to restrict access may appear to be the proper course of action for them to follow. And so be it.

When Barbara and I adopted our daughter Courtney in 1979, the law of the province in which we then resided allowed parents to apprise themselves of basic identifying information that might prove helpful in locating the birthmother of their adopted child at some point in the future. However, the departmental policy was to discourage parents from taking this information, and the law made it difficult to obtain the information at a later stage. Nevertheless, because it was part of the court petition the adopting parents had to sign, it was, for practical purposes, available to them. Being a lawyer, and having worked on the governing legislation, I was in a better position than most adopting parents to understand the implications of the choice we had. If we did not take the opportunity to obtain the information at that point, it would not be available again for many years, and even then only in the event certain conditions were met, not all of which would be within our control.

We were in complete agreement that we should take, record and store as much information as we could from the petition, although we did not at that time have any clear idea what we might do with it, other than to store it in our safety deposit box for future reference. Several years later we were to use that information in a way that resulted in the loving reuniting of Courtney, then ten years old, with her birthmother, and the formation of an extended spiritual family comprising us and our children joined with Courtney's birthmother, her husband and infant daughters. Although we are physically separated by a great distance, the love amongst us is always present. We express gratitude for the strength we were given to look beyond the fears that we heard all around us, both before and after we made the decision to embark on the course we chose. I have given readers only the bare bones of what is a beautifully moving story that will be told in detail at another time. For the moment it serves only to illustrate our freedom to look beyond the law as long as we are not in breach of it.

It is helpful to be able to look at law with an open mind and to ask how it can be used to facilitate the goal you are pursuing, or how you can get around the obstacles it seems to place in your way. Interestingly, that is what many people accept the function of lawyers to be. Often, however, people look at this cynically as "manipulating" the law, because they are suspicious of the goals that are being pursued. When the goal is the expression and extension of love and healing, rather than catering to the temptations of fear and greed, the function takes on a different light, and acquires the character of true service. Rather than allowing ourselves to become upset and angry when the law seems to place an obstacle in our path, we can ask for help to see it differently. Our divine guidance is there to show us the way. I am convinced that there are many in the legal profession who are also there to help, if we can be accepting of our direction and discerning in our choice of helper.

Where the law seems to be inconsistent with our goals and our guidance, and there appears to be no way around the law, for example where it requires us to meet the terms of an award of property or to comply with the terms of a custody or access order that we do not consider to be in anyone's best interests, then we are called upon to look at the conflict this brings up for us. As difficult as it may seem at times to acknowledge, I believe that there is an opportunity for us in every situation, if we look hard enough for it. Because of the emotional strain that surrounds the legal issues that relate to the family, the challenge can be enormous. There is an instinct to fight and to project blame outwardly, rather than to deal with the situation in a loving way. In my experience, however, nothing changes until we first have a little willingness to see differently. Only then does our context open up to miracles.

## CONCLUSION

Trials are but lessons that you failed to learn
presented once again, so where you made a
faulty choice before you now can make a
better one, and thus escape all pain that what
you chose before has brought to you.

*A Course in Miracles*, Text, page 620.

## CHOOSING TO SEE DIFFERENTLY

There may be those who will dismiss this book as imparting the most impractical message they have ever read: "The world just doesn't work that way!" And their world undoubtedly doesn't. And to be perfectly honest to readers, there have been times when I have been tempted myself to doubt the accuracy and/or helpfulness of the perspective I am sharing here. Even as I write, so much that seems to be happening around me, stories of death, destruction and deliberate violence that fill the media, grim interpretations given to these events by other writers and social commentators, and my own personal observations of the inhumanity with which people seem to treat each other at times, test my own commitment to the message of love communicated in the pages of this book. We have as a species a strong attraction to the belief in the objective reality of evil, and that somehow we have to change or control that objective reality if we are to experience peace and security in the world.

From an historical perspective, I find little evidence to convince me that efforts to control "objective reality" have brought much peace and security to the world, but I acknowledge that that is an issue about which reasonable people may disagree. I feel much the same way about the legal system, and about our efforts to use the law and legal process as a tool of social engineering. It seems to be an endless uphill battle to meet the diverse, and often conflicting, expectations people have about the system. Hence my willingness, indeed my eagerness, to find another way of understanding and experiencing how law relates to the events of the world, and how I can make a positive contribution, through law, to a more compassionate world. That way is to recognize that what I see around me are effects of choices that I, and others, make about the kind of world we want to see, and to make those choices on the basis of love, not fear.

My objective has not been to *persuade* readers to make a commitment to seeing law differently, only to remind them that they can choose to do so. Those of you who have stuck with me to this point may see that choice, or may at least be interested in exploring a commitment to change. At the same time, you may be wondering whether it can be done and, if so, how? Does it really make a difference? And to whom?

The doubts we all experience, whether as lawyers, clients, judges, legislators, businesspersons or people who fit into other categories, is that the world does not seem very loving, at least most of the time. If we try to implement our commitment to change, we fear we will be swallowed up in the abyss of a hard-nosed, unforgiving world. We can accept that if everyone made the same commitment it could be a wonderful world, and we could all function quite nicely in it. But we are unable to believe that everyone will make that commitment, at least all at once. And so, while we may be prepared to commit ourselves on condition that sufficient others make the same commitment, we are reluctant to "go it alone." We all feel extremely vulnerable. We feel exposed as pioneers.

Furthermore, most of us feel our commitments to others. As lawyers, many of us are tied to partners and to particular clients. As judges, we have a responsibility to society to uphold justice and the law. As legislators, we represent our constituents; as constitutional reformers, we must uphold either the interests of our province or our nation; as businesspersons, we have the interests of our shareholders and employees to take into account. And most of us have various other interests to think of, not the least of which is the welfare of our families. It is easy to convince ourselves that the choice is not really ours to make after all.

And yet, I believe that the impact of *every* choice I make is felt by others. If I choose to attack someone, the pain is felt by both of us, albeit in different ways. If I choose to love someone, the effect is felt by both of us. And if I choose to heal my conflict, rather than to act it out, the healing I experience can be experienced by others, if they are open to it.

I believe it is fear that traps us in our conventional patterns. We have a lot of trouble trusting others, trusting in ourselves, and trusting in God to provide us with the strength to make the choice and to carry through with it. We have difficulty trusting that our individual choices make a difference. We have trouble listening to our inner guidance, especially in the presence of the fearful voices that seem always to surround us, telling us to do the safe, conventional thing, however hurtful and unloving it may be towards others. And thus, our vision of the world remains limited, closed, fragmented and self-serving.

For me, the first step to seeing law differently was to practice, on a daily basis, being non-judgmental. I did not start with legal issues, because they are generally structured in a way that kindles our attraction to judgment. I started with seemingly less significant items, like how people dress, how they speak, how they drive their cars, how they complain about one another, what they eat, what they write, all of which are experiences we are exposed to day in and day out that seem to irritate us and to bring forth grievances we like to hang onto. We seem to think that by holding grievances against others we will feel better about ourselves. I believe that the opposite is true. Holding onto grievances makes me feel worse. That is because the grievances I hold against others are really projections of feelings I hold about myself, and reflect my own sense of lack of self-worth. In learning to let go of our grievances against others, we can begin to feel better about ourselves.

Law tends to reinforce our grievances about others. Because law carries authority as a social institution, it is easy to use it to legitimize our grievances and to judge the essential worth (i.e. lack of it) of those who transgress its rules. The fear and revulsion that are activated by the horror of some of these transgressions seem to create almost insurmountable barriers to forgiveness. There is a temptation to adopt the most extreme case as the paradigm, to focus on the child killer or the brutal rapist as a justification to dismiss forgiveness as being either an unacceptable or an unattainable spiritual path. My suggestion is again to "start small." Concentrate on legal transgressions that seem less consequential, like traffic misdemeanours, civil negligence, petty theft, writing bad cheques, disorderly conduct and similar offences that do not involve any substantial risk of harm to yourself or others. Practice being non-judgmental and forgiving towards these "offenders," seeing their actions as faulty choices they have made, not as statements about their essential worth. From there it is possible to work upwards to more "serious" offences that strain to engage our judgment reflex.

There is a beautiful story told in *The Forgotten Song* (a video produced to introduce people to *A Course in Miracles*) by a Transylvanian Jew who lost his entire family during the Nazi atrocities of the Second World War. He had avoided a similar fate by misrepresenting himself as a non-Jew and escaping the regime. He tells of the pain and suffering he endured, a lot of it stemming from his feelings of guilt as the sole survivor, and how he was able to overcome it through forgiveness. He describes in moving testimony the peace and healing that his exercises in forgiveness finally brought to him. He tells how he began by forgiving the "little" Nazis, moving on to "bigger" Nazis, until he was finally able to forgive even Hitler, the ultimate symbol of Nazi horror.

Releasing grievances, letting go of judgment and seeing differently are simply different ways of expressing what I have referred to throughout this book as the process of forgiveness. For me it has become both a starting point and an end. It is a process I have committed myself to applying in all of life's situations, not just those involving law and legal process. In my early endeavours to practice forgiveness, I was able to divorce my "private" life from my professional life. Less and less did that make sense to me, as the strength of my commitment increased. It seemed essential to practice forgiveness in all aspects of my life, *especially* in my professional life. This book is, then, in a sense, my manual and my manifesto. Through sharing it, I strengthen my own commitment to the path, and through my commitment the path becomes easier for others, and for me, to travel.

When I boil it down to its essential elements, seeing law differently is for me a matter of attitude and purpose. Law itself can be defined in terms of attitude, a point made by one of the Western world's foremost contemporary legal philosophers, Ronald Dworkin, who concluded his award-winning book *Law's Empire* with this summary:

What is law? Now I offer a different kind of answer. Law is not exhausted by any catalogue of rules or principles, each with its own dominion over some discrete theatre of behavior. Nor by any roster of officials and their powers each over part of our lives. Law's empire is defined by attitude, not territory or power or process. ...It is an interpretative, self-reflective attitude addressed to politics in the broadest sense. It is a protestant attitude that makes each citizen responsible for imagining what his society's public commitments to principle are, and what these commitments require in new circumstances. The protestant character of law is confirmed, and the creative role of private decisions acknowledged, by the backward-looking, judgmental nature of judicial decisions, and also by the regulative assumption that though judges must have the last word, their word is not for that reason the best word. Law's attitude is constructive: it aims, in the interpretative spirit, to lay principle over practice to show the best route to a better future, keeping the right faith with the past. It is, finally, a fraternal attitude, an expression of how we are united in community though divided in project, interest, and conviction. That is, anyway, what law is for us: for the people we want to be and the community we aim to have.[46]

Dworkin, and other legal philosophers, tend to focus on the task of describing, in conceptual terms, what law *is*. To look at law as the expression of attitude, reflecting complex and often

---

[46] Ronald Dworkin, *Law's Empire* (Cambridge, 1986) at p. 413. This book was the winner of the Silver Gavel Award of the American Bar Association. As an aside, I should mention that I had the privilege of studying jurisprudence under Professor Dworkin in my period at Yale Law School in 1965-6.

competing interpretations of purpose, is helpful in demystifying the law. Law has no inherent claim to authority. Rather, it is a reflection of our fears, hopes, beliefs, values and political outlooks, experienced on a range of levels, all struggling for expression in some form of order. To me, however, understanding what law *is* is only helpful if we are prepared to address what law is *for*, and how we are to use it. Those considerations, which also focus on attitude, place law squarely in a functional light.

My vision of law as an expression of attitude invites a commitment to our spiritual unity, and the alignment of our political and social purposes with that commitment. For me, the glory of law's empire is enhanced by our willingness to approach in a loving and peaceful state, not a fearful one, each situation in which we use law. It is about looking for healing in every situation. In an effort to keep me on track, I have adopted six principles, or guidelines, which I would like to share with readers. They are:

- Let go of all grievances I am holding towards the person I am dealing with, whether it be my client, another lawyer, a witness, another party, the judge or the court administrator.

- Never use the law to reinforce a judgment I have made about another person.

- Never use my legal rights or my legal skills to attack another person or to seek vengeance.

- Make all decisions that have legal implications for myself or for someone else while I am in a state of peace, not in a state of fear or anger.

- Trust that the process will open up opportunities for me and for others to make choices that will bring healing, if we make them in a loving, not a fearful state of mind.

- Seek only the justice that is the gift of healing for all who are involved in a legal proceeding.

Equally important is a seventh principle, which helps keep the others in perspective. The seventh is to be aware of my resistance to the other six. I feel this resistance in the temptation that is there continuously to ignore my commitment as I become caught up in the events and engagements of day to day living. The importance of the seventh principle is not that I should feel guilty when I "slip from grace" into anger, impatience, judgment or ingratitude; blaming myself is really no different than blaming someone else. Rather, by training myself to be aware of my emotional reactions, to look at them and see how they misrepresent the truth about who I am and what the nature of my function is in the world and in my profession, I find I can let them go and choose again the way of peace. The resistance I experience attests to the power of the six principles, if I simply choose to let them guide me.

It was through the willingness of Victor Hugo's Bishop to see beyond appearances and past experiences, and to look upon the present with a mind attuned to love and acceptance, that Jean Valjean was able to see beyond his own illusions to recognize the beautiful person that he was, and to go on to touch the lives of others in a loving way. There is, I believe, a "ripple effect" in everything we do, in every choice we make.[47] Through our choosing to see differently, others are enabled to make a better choice, whether in similar or in different circumstances. No one can make our choices for us, and no one can "fix" our world for us. Seeing law differently, and seeing the world differently, are our own areas of responsibility. The choice resides with each of us, and I believe each of us has the inherent strength to make that choice, if we choose to call upon that strength.

In the end, my message is about choice: *choosing* to see differently. It is as practical, or as impractical, as that! The commitment to seeing differently leads to other choices, each one presenting the opportunity to move ahead, or to turn back temporarily. Some choices bring more healing than others, to ourselves and to others, but we need not be deterred by a "faulty" choice from making a "better" one at the next opportunity.

Writing this book was a choice I made; reading it was a choice you made. I choose to see our coming together in this way as an opportunity for healing in the legal profession and in the world.

---

[47] The 45th "miracle principle" of *A Course in Miracles*, Text, p.4, states that a miracle "may touch many people you have not even met, and produce undreamed of changes in situations of which you are not even aware."